Critical Acclaim for Dana Yeaton's
Mad River Rising

"Dana Yeaton's play is revealed to be a compelling—often funny, sometimes tender—chronicle of a deep personal struggle for identity. . . . Yeaton's characters are very personal and real—and thus powerful. . . . an engaging and moving play."

—Times Argus

"*Rising* is a play of universal appeal. . . . It will find a wide audience."

—The Burlington Free Press

"[*Mad River Rising*] represents Yeaton's achieved mastery of the medium, a play for all seasons and all locales. The generational tensions that it explores, as well as the cultural prejudices it exposes, have the correct balance between the particular and the general to strike chords of recognition in any audience, much the way *Our Town* has. The play is moving without being either obvious or saccharine. It is also as economical of speech and as dry of wit as the people whom it portrays. . . . It is also an eminently theatrical play, sliding between now and the past and mixing characters of various generations as in a dream."

—Shelburne News

Midwives

A play by Dana Yeaton

Adapted from the bestselling novel
Midwives by Chris Bohjalian

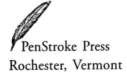

PenStroke Press
Rochester, Vermont

PenStroke Press
118 Main Street
Rochester, Vermont 05767

PenStroke Press is a student publishing venture established in Rochester High School, in partnership with Inner Traditions International and Schenkman Books, funded by the Randolph Regional School-to-Work Consortium.

Copyright © 2000 by Dana Yeaton

Library of Congress Cataloguing-in-Publication Data available
ISBN 0-9669177-3-1

10 9 8 7 6 5 4 3 2 1
Printed and bound in Canada by Webcom

This book was typeset in Garamond
Text design by Erica Andrews, Sarah Blair, and Jenny Jacques
Typesetting and layout by Holli Bushnell, Emily Mendell, and Andrew Torsnes
Production editorial staff: Holli Bushnell, Jeanie Levitan, Jessica Matthews, and Emily Mendell
Cover design by Peri Champine

PenStroke Press books are distributed by Schenkman Books, 118 Main Street, Rochester, Vermont 05767 • (802) 767-3702 • schenkma@sover.net

For my mother—and Chris's biggest fan—
Sally Witman

ACKNOWLEDGMENTS

Thanks to the friends and colleagues who have been early readers of this script: Kathy Blume, Ethan Bowen, Erin Carr, Frankie Dunleavy, Molly Fitzgibbon, Harry McEnerny, Mark Jacobson, Connan Morrissey, Mark Nash, and Carol Warnock. Thanks to Castleton State College, the White River Valley Players, and the South Hero Players for supporting the production of *Midwives* before there was a script and to my editor, Jeanie Levitan, and her staff for their tireless attention to detail *and* the big picture. Special thanks to Blake Robison, whose ongoing support for my work has made such a difference. Finally, thanks to Chris Bohjalian for trusting me with this brilliant and original story.

Midwives was commissioned with a grant from the Arts Endowment Fund of Vermont. In the fall of 2000, Vermont Stage Company will give the play its professional premiere as part of the Catherine Filene Shouse New Play Series, which fosters the development of new plays and playwrights for the American theatre. The Catherine Filene Shouse New Play Series is dedicated to the memory of Mrs. Shouse, a philanthropist and lifelong supporter of the arts.

CAST OF CHARACTERS
(for 9 or more performers)

Women

Sibyl Danforth

Connie Danforth

Charlotte Bedford, Rita

Anne Austin, Lori Pine, Maggie, Photographer, Miss Martin

Louise, Molly, Dr. Gerson, Court Reporter, Phone Woman, Foreman

Men

Defense Attorney Stephen Hastings, Dr. Barton Hewitt

State's Attorney Tanner, Timothy, Forensic Specialist

Reverend Asa Bedford, Joe, Dr. Lang, Coroner Tierney, Physician

David Pine, Road Crew Man, Dr. Dummond, Judge Dorset

SETTING: An outpatient room, empty except for two chairs—a cushioned, medical recliner and a waiting room chair. Transitions to other locations—bedrooms, office, kitchen, and courtroom—should be as immediate as possible.

ACT 1

AT RISE: SIBYL sits connected to an IV, reading a large cloth-covered book. She notices the AUDIENCE. Awkward pause.

SIBYL. We're just waiting for my daughter. Then we'll start. *(Returns to her reading for a moment, then to AUDIENCE.)* She's going to be a doctor so she's probably working on her "running late" skills. To me, it's a sign, but then of course, I grew up in the '60s when everything was a sign. "Life is a metaphor for life." I actually wrote that in here. It's funny, I used to worry that someone would read my journal; for a while, it was my worst fear. Now I worry no one will bother.

Running late is no accident, though. People arrive when they arrive for a reason. Like babies. I'm not saying Connie doesn't love me, she does, I've never doubted that. . . . Rarely doubted that. She's growing up, I can't expect to be the focus of her life. My active mothering days are over, have been since . . . the trial, really. So I'm not her hero anymore. It's my job to grow up too. *(Looks at IV.)* And soon.

(Tries to return to reading. Suddenly:)

But it's impossible to stop mothering. You can't just watch your child clam up and disappear and then she starts making life decisions based on— Nine years is a very long time to carry something around inside. It's like stillbirth, the way I thought of it as a kid: "You mean she's *still* giving birth?" "Oh yeah, she's in her third year of labor." Of course a doctor would just grab a pair of forceps, go in there, and get that baby out. We midwives like to let things take their own time, let the mother do the work. We're just there to catch. That doesn't mean we don't have tricks to get things going, though.

CONNIE. *(Entering.)* Mom.

SIBYL. Sweetie!

CONNIE. I am so sorry.

SIBYL. *(Referring to the IV.)* It's okay, I started without you.

CONNIE. It was ridiculous this morning. Four and a half *hours* to get up here.

SIBYL. I'm glad you made the trip.

CONNIE. Oh come on, what am I gonna do, not come? You look great.

SIBYL. You're just saying that because I still have hair.

CONNIE. No. Really. Where's the doctor?

SIBYL. I believe he was called away on an emergency cruise.

CONNIE. Well who is here? Someone should be monitoring you.

SIBYL. Sit. Relax. There's a very pleasant woman named Louise who said she'd be back in a moment. . . . Sweetie, you're here now. You're not in the car. Sit. I want to congratulate you.

CONNIE. On what?

SIBYL. On this. *(She holds out a letter.)*

CONNIE. Oh, this is nothing.

SIBYL. A letter from financial aid at the Boston University School of Medicine is nothing?

CONNIE. It wasn't supposed to come to you.

SIBYL. Give me a hug! *(To AUDIENCE.)* I like to make contact with the mother right away, get a sense of where she is physically. *(To CONNIE.)* I am so proud of you. . . . When did you find out, why didn't you tell me?

CONNIE. I just— I hadn't decided. I still haven't.

SIBYL. You're not going?

CONNIE. No, I'm thinking about it. I have a little time and . . . I wanted to talk to you first. See what you think.

SIBYL. I think it's wonderful.

CONNIE. I mean how you feel about it. Really.

SIBYL. I just told you.

CONNIE. Mom, I would be studying to be an ob-gyn.

SIBYL. That's what I . . . assumed. And I'm thrilled.

CONNIE. I knew you'd do this.

SIBYL. What?

CONNIE. Pretend to be all happy and supportive.

SIBYL. I am happy and supportive, if that's what you want. Is that what you want?

CONNIE. Mom, you hate hospitals.

SIBYL. I'm not particularly comfortable—

CONNIE. You hate hospitals and you hate doctors and you *should* hate hospitals and doctors.

SIBYL. That's not true. There's Dr. Pete, Dr. Fillian, there's Barton, whom I adore. Even my oncologist is not a bad person, when he's in the country.

CONNIE. See. You can't even pretend. I would be one of the bad guys, Mom, with florescent lights, and drug company samples, and malpractice insurance.

SIBYL. Honey, if I'd had malpractice you wouldn't be the financial aid poster child. Let me ask you a question. And you have to be truthful, okay?

CONNIE. 'Kay.

SIBYL. *(To AUDIENCE.)* You watch. This should get her started. *(To CONNIE.)* Your decision to become a doctor, is it because of—

CONNIE. I haven't decided yet.

SIBYL. Your decision to look into becoming a doctor, okay? . . . Is it because of what happened to Charlotte?

> *(Cut to court scene. Note: Courtroom*
> *excerpts appear in italics.)*

STATE'S ATTORNEY TANNER. So you asked the Reverend Bedford to bring you a knife?

SIBYL. Yes.

TANNER. You didn't just ask for any knife. You asked for a sharp knife, didn't you?

SIBYL. I don't think I would have asked for a dull one.

TANNER. *Both the Reverend Bedford and your apprentice recall you asking for "the sharpest knife in the house." Were those your words?*

SIBYL. *Those might have been my words.*

TANNER. *Is the reason you needed "the sharpest knife in the house" because you don't carry a scalpel?*

SIBYL. *Of course I don't. I've never met a midwife who does.*

TANNER. *Is that because a midwife is not a surgeon?*

SIBYL. *Yes.*

TANNER. *Do you believe that surgeons possess a special expertise that you as a midwife do not?*

SIBYL. *Good Lord, don't you think so?*

TANNER. *Mrs. Danforth?*

SIBYL. *Yes. Surgeons know things I don't. So do airline pilots and kindergarten teachers.*

CONNIE. No. It's not about that, any of that . . . It's more about you.

SIBYL. That's what I was afraid of.

CONNIE. Why?

SIBYL. I was hoping your decision would have more to do with you than me.

CONNIE. It *is* about me. Think about how I grew up. What I was exposed to. It's probably in my DNA.

SIBYL. Just because you're genetically predisposed doesn't mean you should spend the rest of your life catching babies.

CONNIE. So you don't actually want me to go?

SIBYL. No, I'm saying—

LOUISE. *(Entering.)* How ya comin' in here?

SIBYL. Louise, this is my daughter, Connie.

LOUISE. We met in the hall.

SIBYL. Did I mention Connie is going to be a doctor?

LOUISE. Really, what kind?

CONNIE. Evil.

LOUISE. Too bad there's already a glut. You comfortable?

SIBYL. I'm fine.

CONNIE. Is there an oncologist here now?

LOUISE. God, I hope so. We're the Oncology Wing. *(To SIBYL.)* Something to drink?

SIBYL. No, thanks.

LOUISE. If you need me, I'll just be around the corner.

CONNIE. Excuse me. . . . I'm just wondering, who's in charge of my mother's case right now.

LOUISE. Besides me?

CONNIE. I just mean in terms of . . .

LOUISE. Look, this isn't open heart surgery, this is chemo. The chart says how much, that's how much she gets. . . . I mean, I don't mean to be rude or—

CONNIE. No, I'm sorry.

LOUISE. Don't be sorry. She's your mother. . . . If you want to talk to someone, Dr. Farr should be back in a few minutes.

CONNIE. Thank you. *(LOUISE exits.)* Well, she's . . .

SIBYL. She is, isn't she?

CONNIE. Have you met this Dr. Farr? Do you know anything about him?

SIBYL. Her. She seemed nice. She does that doctor trip where they pretend to have all the time in the world. I think they actually lower their heart rates, so you feel all cared for, even though they're the *cure* people. They have other people around for the time-consuming *care* part. . . . I'm doing it again, aren't I? Must be the toxins, I'm not really like this. . . . What? . . . Now you're laughing at me.

CONNIE. Renegade.

SIBYL. What?

CONNIE. You don't remember this? They asked you in court about your "Question Authority" bumper sticker and if you saw yourself as a renegade.

SIBYL. What did I say?

CONNIE. "I prefer to think of myself as a pioneer."

SIBYL. Oh, God.

CONNIE. I know.

SIBYL. . . . So what are we arguing about?

CONNIE. We're not arguing.

SIBYL. Discussing.

CONNIE. You were trying to talk me out of becoming an ob-gyn by pretending to encourage me.

SIBYL. That's not true. I just don't want you to become something because you think you should.

CONNIE. How can you say that? I have always wanted to be a baby-catcher.

SIBYL. Always? *(To AUDIENCE.)* Watch. This should get her rushing.

CONNIE. Since, I can't remember when.

SIBYL. "Why is she being so mean?"

CONNIE. That was my first!

SIBYL. "Shouldn't he do the other one too?"

CONNIE. I was seven! (*During the following, LORI PINE and her husband, DAVID, roll in a brightly colored birthing bed. DAVID rubs his wife's back and legs. SIBYL lights a candle.*)

SIBYL. Connie's dad died when she was two; he was an animal lover who ended up sharing the front seat of his Datsun with a moose. After that, when a mother was in labor I could always leave Connie next door with the Pine's, which was a perfect system, except, of course, when Lori Pine was the woman in labor . . .

LORI. Oh, God. Please.

DAVID. Deep and slow.

LORI. Something's wrong.

SIBYL. You're doing just fine.

LORI. I can't do it.

DAVID. You've done it before, honey.

LORI. It wasn't like this. It never hurt like this.

DAVID. That's what you said last time, remember?

SIBYL. And you were wonderful. . . . Deep and slow now. (*CONNIE, age seven, enters, eating a rice cake. She watches, entranced.*) That rush you're feeling is not pain, all right? It is a very interesting sensation that needs all of your attention.

DAVID. Should we try some more tea?

LORI. I don't want more tea.

DAVID. It's supposed to help get you started again.

LORI. I know!

CONNIE. Why is she being so mean?

DAVID. Connie!

LORI. What did she say?

DAVID. She said you must be in transition.

LORI. No, what did she say?

CONNIE. Are you mad at Mr. Pine?

LORI. No, sweetie. I'm just feeling cranky.

DAVID. Mrs. Pine is doing her impression of a bear.

LORI. Shut up and gimme a kiss. *(They kiss.)*

DAVID. Big, loving mama bear. *(Kiss.)*

SIBYL. Sweetie, Mommy needs you to be in the other room now.

CONNIE. I want to see.

LORI. Sibyl, it's fine.

SIBYL. You sure?

LORI. I'm sure. We can use the fresh air. . . . Oh boy.

DAVID. Here comes.

SIBYL. All right, you two, I want a little more of that smoochy stuff, okay? Helps to prime the pump. *(To AUDIENCE.)* I know it sounds touchy-feely, but it's true. You want the juices flowing. With Lori, the rushes were there, she was fully dilated, but nothing was happening. She had the pain, but no urge to push.

LORI. Maybe we should go to the hospital.

SIBYL. You're doing just fine.

LORI. I can't do it.

DAVID. You *are* doing it, babe.

LORI. Something's wrong this time.

SIBYL. Okay folks, we're gonna try something else. It's heavy petting time.

DAVID. This is that chemical thing, right?

SIBYL. Someone's been doing his reading.

LORI. What?

DAVID. She wants me to stimulate your breasts. It triggers this chemical.

SIBYL. Oxytocin. It's an endocrine hormone that speeds up labor.

LORI. Well, I've always been a big supporter of hormones.

SIBYL. . . . Beats an IV, doesn't it? . . . Hmmm. Feels better in here already.

CONNIE. . . . Shouldn't he do the other one too?

DAVID. Are you still here?

SIBYL. Actually, she's right. Two hands on the wheel, Mr. Pine. Don't want that baby popping out lopsided, do you?

DAVID. Is that better?

LORI. . . . That's better . . . yeah.

CONNIE. . . . Is it working?

SIBYL. We'll see. . . . I'll be back in just a minute, okay?

CONNIE. Will I be back? . . . Mommy? *(SIBYL and CONNIE return to the hospital room.)*

SIBYL. *(To AUDIENCE.)* There, that wasn't so bad.

LORI. *(off)* Sibyl, I want to push now!

CONNIE. About six pushes later, there was little Jonathan Pine. Six pounds eight ounces.

SIBYL. You remember.

CONNIE. Of course I remember. Lori let me stroke the soft spot on his little head and he looked up at me with those puppy eyes, and I said to him, "Welcome to the world."

SIBYL. *(To AUDIENCE.)* That *was* a productive little rush.

CONNIE. And afterward, when David was holding him, I counted his toes and got up to eleven. Remember?

SIBYL. I do. But, of course, I cheated. . . . Look.

CONNIE. What?

SIBYL. *(To AUDIENCE.)* Here goes. Time to break the waters. *(SIBYL holds up the cloth-covered book.)* I thought this might interest you.

TANNER. Is a cesarean section a surgical procedure?

SIBYL. Obviously.

TANNER. Do you think you're qualified to perform this surgery?

SIBYL. In my worst nightmares, I never imagined I'd have to.

TANNER. I'll repeat my question. Do you think you are qualified to perform this surgery?

SIBYL. No, and I've never said I was.

TANNER. And yet you did. With a kitchen knife, on a living woman, you brutally—

STEPHEN HASTINGS. Objection!

SIBYL. You're welcome to keep it.

CONNIE. But it's your journal.

SIBYL. I won't be needing it much, though.

CONNIE. Mother, don't be morbid.

SIBYL. I didn't say I'm checking out tomorrow. It's just, I realized something today when I was looking— Can I read you something?

CONNIE. Sure.

SIBYL. "Clarissa Roberson was laboring away in her bed this morning and there was her mother, Maureen, right beside me, helping her daughter through it. It was a long labor and Maureen must be close to sixty, but she was rubbing and breathing and lifting and laughing, doing everything she could. Most mothers are happy brewing their daughters tea or cheering them on from the headboard. At one point between rushes I put the baby oil down to check the fetal heart-rate and there's Maureen, up to her elbows in oil massaging her little girl's perineum. It was beautiful. Incredibly beautiful, and I thought, maybe I'll do that one day."

CONNIE. That's lovely.

SIBYL. I always thought I was writing these secret notes to myself for when I was older, and then I cracked it open today—first time in, must be almost ten years. The more I read, the more I— I just got the feeling that all that time I'd actually been writing this for you. *(She offers CONNIE the journal.)*

CONNIE. Mom, no.

SIBYL. I want you to have it.

CONNIE. You should finish it. Don't you want to keep going?

SIBYL. I've given up writing. I'm old enough now, if I want to talk to myself I just do it out loud. That way there's no record of phrases like "groove together" and "fight the establishment." By the way, I often used the word "stoned" in here to mean a high feeling, not necessarily drug-induced.

CONNIE. Wait a minute. What about your first birth?

SIBYL. I was the only straight person there. That's how I was elected midwife.

CONNIE. Right.

SIBYL. It's true. I was pregnant with you. Your father and all the other men suddenly remember their genetic codes: Must get help. I'm left there with the mother and . . . God, what was her name?

CONNIE. Who?

SIBYL. This friend of ours. Tripping her brains out.

CONNIE. Doesn't matter.

SIBYL. Luna Raskin.

CONNIE. Luna?

SIBYL. Every time the poor mother has a contraction Luna screams, "They're killing her! They're killing her!"

CONNIE. Great.

SIBYL. I thought she was talking about the rushes, but it turned out she was convinced that Lyndon Johnson and Dean Rusk were torturing this woman. . . . Go ahead. Read me a section, while I finish my [IV] cocktail here.

CONNIE. I don't want to get all serious.

SIBYL. It's not *all* serious.

CONNIE. I know but . . . okay, I'll read something from before.

SIBYL. I was looking at the one where I felt you flutter inside me for the first time.

CONNIE. "Lonely births are the saddest things in the world. They can bring me down for days. Charlotte . . . " I'll find another.

SIBYL. It's all right.

CONNIE. This is not going to cheer us up.

SIBYL. Go ahead.

CONNIE. "Charlotte Bedford's birth might be a lonely one. She's from Alabama, so Asa and their little boy, Foogie, are her only family within fifteen hundred miles. She's met very few people outside of Asa's parish, and they tend to keep a certain respectful distance since she's the new preacher's wife. In fact, I may be her only friend up here and so her prenatal visits go on forever."

(SIBYL'S office. CHARLOTTE admires photos on the wall.)

CHARLOTTE. Oh my, look at her. Isn't she precious?

SIBYL. Michelle Trombley.

CHARLOTTE. What's that she's wrapped in?

SIBYL. It's lovely, isn't it? Mrs. Trombley is a fiber artist. I have one of her shawls, that's how she paid me for catching Michelle here.

CHARLOTTE. I hope all these women don't try to pay you in shawls.

SIBYL. Oh no. I have all sorts of mothers. Let me see. . . . School teacher. . . . Clarinetist. . . . Newspaper editor. . . . She grooms dogs. . . . Waitress.

CHARLOTTE. What about her?

SIBYL. Ski instructor.

CHARLOTTE. Very outdoorsy. . . . Like this one.

SIBYL. She and her husband run a vegetable farm. Let me see, I've got a celebrity here somewhere . . .

CHARLOTTE. They all look so healthy.

SIBYL. Well so did you, I bet, when you had Foogie.

CHARLOTTE. I don't think so, I—

SIBYL. Here she is, the first female commissioner of travel and tourism.

CHARLOTTE. You could start your own little civilization here. One of everything.

SIBYL. Except for bankers.

CHARLOTTE. No bankers?

SIBYL. And no lawyers.

CHARLOTTE. Well, for now maybe. But that might change. Did you ever think you'd have a preacher's wife?

SIBYL. Actually . . . *(Pointing to a picture.)*

CHARLOTTE. No.

SIBYL. And here. You're my third.

CHARLOTTE. Sibyl, if you can get three preachers to agree on something you can certainly get a banker and a lawyer up on this wall.

SIBYL. That still leaves the impossible dream . . .

CHARLOTTE. Oh, I don't know. I believe anybody can change their mind over time.

SIBYL. . . . Even an ob-gyn? *(CONNIE interrupts the scene by handing SIBYL the journal.)*

CONNIE. See, this is what I don't particularly want to do.

SIBYL. What?

CONNIE. I object to the implication that a doctor necessarily doesn't have a soul.

SIBYL. I would never say that.

CONNIE. You just finished telling me—

SIBYL. And before that I said I know wonderful doctors. I know you. You have a soul.

CONNIE. I'm not a doctor.

SIBYL. Why not?

CONNIE. Besides the fact that I've only *applied* to med school?

SIBYL. And been accepted. What keeps you from just accepting them? I hope it's not my opinion.

CONNIE. Is that so bad, it matters to me what you think? Most parents would kill for this opportunity.

SIBYL. I once asked my mother if she thought I should marry your dad. Know what she said?

CONNIE. No?

SIBYL. "If you have to ask, you better not." . . . Pissed me off so much I married him.

CONNIE. So is that your advice?

SIBYL. *(Holding out the journal.)* This is my advice.

CONNIE. Mom.

SIBYL. It will give you some perspective.

CONNIE. Just tell me. What is it in there that you want me to know? Can you just summarize? Or point me to the page?

SIBYL. I want you to know what happened.

CONNIE. A tragedy happened. I know that.

SIBYL. I want it to stop happening . . . and that won't occur until you know what took place in that room.

CONNIE. And I'm telling you I do.

SIBYL. How could you? Connie, you weren't there.

CONNIE. I know more than you think. Can we leave it at that?

SIBYL. No.

CONNIE. All right. . . . I know that it started March 14, 1981. *(As CONNIE speaks, SIBYL enters a birthing scene with apprentice ANNE AUSTIN, CHARLOTTE, and her husband, ASA BEDFORD.)* I know that the first stage of Charlotte's labor was uneventful, but that it had lasted much longer than anyone would have expected. It was just before midnight, almost thirteen hours in, when you decided to break Charlotte's waters.

ANNE. I don't understand why you just did that.

SIBYL. She's dilated eight centimeters. The baby's head is engaged. . . . It was time.

CONNIE. That was when it started. A slow drizzle that turned to ice the instant it landed.

CHARLOTTE. Asa!

ASA. I'm here, Charlotte.

CHARLOTTE. I can't do this.

SIBYL. You're doing fine.

CHARLOTTE. It's not like the last time.

ASA. It is, Charlotte. You can do it.

SIBYL. Actually, from what Charlotte told me about having Foogie, there is a difference. This baby's in the posterior position; the back of its head is up against your spine. Last time you delivered—

CHARLOTTE. He.

SIBYL. Pardon?

ASA. Charlotte believes the child is a boy.

CHARLOTTE. I know it's a boy.

SIBYL. Well, apparently your little boy doesn't want to miss a thing. He's facing sunny side up.

CHARLOTTE. Oh, God. He's tearing me apart inside.

SIBYL. Well let's get you on all fours and see if we can persuade this little fella to face the other way and give his mom a break.

ASA. *(Quietly.)* Holy Father, please help Your child, Charlotte Bedford, through this ordeal. Give her the strength and the courage to endure what is to come. Protect her and guide us here tonight that we may bring another of Your children safely into this world.

ANNE. Sibyl, what can I do?

SIBYL. You have to want this.

ANNE. Want what?

SIBYL. I meant Charlotte. . . . Let's have another hot compress. Okay, Charlotte, your body knows what it's doing, you just have to trust, all right. Let yourself relax and open.

CHARLOTTE. I want to push.

SIBYL. Very soon.

CHARLOTTE. I can't do this. I'm not strong enough.

SIBYL. That is not true. That pain you're feeling *is* your strength. Do you hear? That's a life force in you. Now you pay attention to it.

CHARLOTTE. It hurts even when I don't have a contraction.

ASA. Say it with me, Charlotte. "Our Father . . ." Say it with me.

ASA & CHARLOTTE. "Our Father, who art in heaven, hallowed be thy name, thy kingdom come, thy will be—"

CHARLOTTE. Asa!

ASA. I'm here.

CHARLOTTE. I'm not gonna make it.

SIBYL. You are. You're doing it.

ANNE. She's scared.

SIBYL. Put the compress on her neck. Charlotte, listen, this is hard. Back labor is normally longer and it can be very, very hard. But it is not fatal. Do you understand? . . . Charlotte?

ASA. She understands.

SIBYL. We don't like that position, we try something else, all right? Asa, come up here on your knees and support her. Charlotte, you just lean back, that's it, let him take your weight. Good. *(Pulling on latex gloves.)* Now let's see if that little fella is any closer to making his entrance.

TANNER. And was Charlotte Bedford fully dilated at that time?

SIBYL. Very nearly.

TANNER. Was she fully *dilated?*

SIBYL. She was nine centimeters.

TANNER. And what is considered full dilation?

SIBYL. Ten.

TANNER. So despite the fact that she was not yet fully dilated, you instructed her to push, is that right?

SIBYL. *It's common practice with women who have already given birth.*

TANNER. *Despite her discomfort?*

SIBYL. *Mr. Tanner, most women who've experienced labor expect there to be some discomfort.*

> (CHARLOTTE shrieks in pain, heaving her body almost off the bed. SIBYL catches her.)

SIBYL. Whoa.

ANNE. *(Looking down, horrified.)* Sibyl . . . *(The sheet has a large circle of blood. SIBYL calmly takes CHARLOTTE'S pulse.)*

SIBYL. Charlotte, we're going to take a little break from pushing now, all right?

ASA. *(Referring to the blood.)* Is that normal?

CHARLOTTE. What?

SIBYL. We have some bloody show. Anne, why don't we get a blood pressure reading?

STEPHEN HASTINGS. *And what did you find?*

SIBYL. *It had dropped to 90 over 60. Charlotte's pulse was up into the 100s.*

STEPHEN HASTINGS. *And did you monitor the baby's heart-rate at that time?*

SIBYL. *(Puts on her fetalscope, listens to the child.) Of course. It was as infrequent as 90 beats per minute.*

STEPHEN HASTINGS. *And what action did you take?*

SIBYL. *I continued to monitor both mother and child. I decided that if her blood pressure continued to drop, or if there were signs of shock, or fetal distress, I would have Anne call the town rescue squad and move Charlotte to the hospital. (To ANNE.)* How we doing?

ANNE. Seventy-five over fifty.

SIBYL. I'm only getting a heart rate of sixty-five a minute. . . . Go ahead. *(ANNE exits.)*

ASA. What's wrong?

CHARLOTTE. I knew it.

SIBYL. Listen, the bleeding has almost stopped.

ASA. Then where did she go?

SIBYL. To make a call. The vital signs are lower than I like to see them at home. . . . I want to have Dr. Hewitt take a look.

CHARLOTTE. In the hospital?

ASA. If she's not bleeding, what's wrong?

SIBYL. There's a chance that the placenta is detaching itself from the wall of the uterus. Dr. Hewitt has seen many of my mothers under circumstances—

ANNE. *(off)* Sibyl! . . . It's dead.

ASA. What?

ANNE. The phone has gone dead.

TANNER. And why did you not use the phone in the bedroom?

SIBYL. I didn't want to . . . alarm the Bedfords.

TANNER. Weren't you alarmed?

SIBYL. No, I was concerned. But I was making an effort to keep myself in check for—

TANNER. You were calling an ambulance to rush this poor woman to the hospital and you were not alarmed?

ASA. *(Holding the phone.)* This one is dead, too. *(Pause. The sound of FREEZING RAIN.)*

ANNE. What are we going to do?

SIBYL. Obviously, we'll take her in my station wagon. She can spread out in the back.

ASA. It's freezing rain out there.

SIBYL. Is it? When did that start?

ANNE. An hour and a half ago.

SIBYL. Well, I'm a local girl, I learned to drive on this stuff. Anne, can you bring the car up to the door? . . . What?

ANNE. Is it an automatic?

(Pause. Now what?)

ASA. I can do it.

SIBYL. My keys are downstairs in my—

CHARLOTTE. No, Asa. Please.

ASA. I'll just be gone a minute.

CHARLOTTE. No. Please don't go. . . . Please.

SIBYL. Okay, okay. Asa's not going anywhere. Listen, Anne will stay here with you, all right? I'm just gonna bring the car up and then we'll get you to the hospital, all right? *(CHARLOTTE nods.)* I'll be right back. *(To ANNE, calming her.)* Stay with the vitals. Okay?

ANNE. I'm fine.

ASA. Be careful on the steps.

STEPHEN HASTINGS. *Please tell us what you encountered when you stepped outside.*

SIBYL. *Well, the ground.*

STEPHEN HASTINGS. *You fell.*

SIBYL. *Immediately. It was glare ice, I— I tried to shuffle along but, I fell several more times.*

STEPHEN HASTINGS. *How many?*

SIBYL. *I think I counted four.*

STEPHEN HASTINGS. *Were you injured?*

SIBYL. *Yes. I sprained my ankle and later I found that I had bruised both knees and my elbow.*

STEPHEN HASTINGS. *The pictures taken three days later show lacerations on the fingers and palms of both hands. Was that from falling?*

SIBYL. *No, I gave up walking to the car. I ended up crawling most of the way. It was even worse on the way back. (SIBYL returns, limping.)*

ANNE. Sibyl, what happened?

ASA. Are you all right?

SIBYL. I'm fine I— I'm afraid the car slid off the— Well, it's not going anywhere.

ASA. Sit down.

SIBYL. How's our mother doing?

CHARLOTTE. I believe I am fine now, Sibyl.

ANNE. It's amazing. The bleeding has stopped. Completely. Her blood pressure is back up.

ASA. Tell her about the baby.

ANNE. Its heart-rate is back up to one-twenty.

CHARLOTTE. *His* heart-rate.

SIBYL. That's wonderful. Look at you, you've got your complexion back. . . . You're not clammy.

ANNE. We prayed, Sibyl. All three of us.

CHARLOTTE. And it worked.

SIBYL. Well then . . . let's get that little boy out of you.

CONNIE. According to testimony, it was just after 2:00 A.M. when you had Charlotte resume pushing. The baby hadn't yet turned during its descent and you knew the back of its head would continue causing Charlotte pain as it pushed its way through her pelvis. By now, you were concerned about fetal distress but you reminded yourself that Charlotte would have to lose six or seven pints of blood before she'd be in real danger of cardiac arrest.

SIBYL. *(To CHARLOTTE.)* Little more. Little more. That's it, little more.

ANNE. You're doing fine.

ASA. You are great, Charlotte. You are the best.

SIBYL. 'Nother second. 'Nother second. That's it. 'Nother second. . . *(Finally CHARLOTTE exhales.)* Yes!

TANNER. Would you please recall for us, to the best of your ability, what you said to Charlotte Bedford during that time?

ANNE. I told her she was doing fine.

ASA. I believe I said she was the best. That I loved her.

TANNER. Did you ever specifically encourage her to continue pushing?

ASA. I don't believe I did.

ANNE. No.

TANNER. Why not?

ASA. I was deferring to the experts, I suppose.

ANNE. I assumed that was Sibyl's decision. To decide how long Mrs. Bedford should push before . . .

TANNER. *Before what?*

ANNE. *Before it would be dangerous.*

CHARLOTTE. I can't do it, Asa. I'm too weak.

ASA. You can.

CHARLOTTE. Every time I push, it's like a knife. . . . This is killing pain.

SIBYL. Why don't we take a break from pushing.

CHARLOTTE. . . . Oh God.

ASA. It's just a break, Charlotte.

ANNE. You're doing fine.

SIBYL. And your baby's definitely making progress. Can you feel it?

CHARLOTTE. He is?

SIBYL. We'll just give you a few minutes to get your strength up.

CHARLOTTE. I don't have any, Sibyl.

SIBYL. We'll see how you feel after a break.

CONNIE. She rested for nearly half an hour, while you monitored her signs and tried to buck up everyone's spirits. Not just the Bedfords' but Anne Austin's too. Just after three you had her start pushing again, but by four in the morning, Charlotte was clearly exhausted and you could see that her confidence was failing.

SIBYL. 'Nother second. Little more, and . . . good! Good, Charlotte. Let's stop for a little while.

ASA. You're doing great. . . . Hey, what's the matter?

CHARLOTTE. I told you. I told you all. I can't do it.

SIBYL. Well, your baby seems to think you can. He just has to clear the pubic bone and he'll be crowning. What do you say to that? . . . Charlotte?

ASA. She's just catching her breath.

CHARLOTTE. I'm not! I'm . . . I'm telling you, I have nothing left. I can't push this baby out. I don't have the—

SIBYL. Charlotte, listen to me. I have birthed over five hundred babies in my life, and I have never seen a woman any stronger or work any harder than you. Do you understand me?

TANNER. And was that a true statement?

SIBYL. Yes. She worked as hard as any woman I had ever seen.

TANNER. You had never seen a woman stronger than Charlotte Bedford? A woman who had lost a large quantity of blood? Who had been in labor for 18 hours? Who was now in her . . . fifth hour of pushing?

SIBYL. I was referring to the strength of her determination.

TANNER. I see. So you were not referring to her physical strength, is that right?

SIBYL. No. That's not right.

TANNER. You were referring to her physical strength.

SIBYL. I don't make the distinction between what someone is physically capable of and what they believe.

TANNER. Mrs. Danforth, at four-thirty on the morning of March 15, 1981, did you believe that Charlotte Bedford had the strength—physical, emotional, spiritual, whatever kind of strength it takes—to deliver that baby?

> *(SIBYL walks slowly to a bedroom window and looks out.)*

ANNE. Sibyl?

SIBYL. I thought I heard a truck. . . . Did anyone hear a sand truck? *(ASA and ANNE exchange a look.)*

CHARLOTTE. I'm ready, Sibyl. . . . I want to push again. *(Coaching resumes.)*

ROAD CREW MAN. *No sir, after two A.M. we didn't send a truck out 'til, must have been six-thirty, quarter of seven.*

STEPHEN HASTINGS. *And why was that?*

ROAD CREW MAN. *It was nothing but glass out there. Even the main roads, when I finally got to 'em, I was just crawlin' along, top of that center line, didn't dare get in my own lane or I'da slid off into the ditch.*

STEPHEN HASTINGS. *Were there any other vehicles on the road that morning?*

ROAD CREW MAN. *Oh yeah, quite a few. 'Cept they were all in ditches. Wasn't anything movin' 'fore we got there with the sand.*

ASA. I can see his head!

SIBYL. We're in the home stretch, folks.

ANNE. Yes!

SIBYL. Come on, Charlotte, you can do it, you can do it, can do it—

ANNE. That's it, you're doing it. You're doing it, Charlotte—

TANNER. *Did you really believe she was capable of delivering that child?*

SIBYL. Can do it, can-do-it, can-do-it. *(To TANNER.)* Yes! *(To CHARLOTTE.)* Do-it, do-it, do-it—

ASA. He's coming now, Charlotte. He's coming.

ANNE. You're doing great, Charlotte. You're pushing that little boy out.

TANNER. *Is it standard practice for midwives to lie to their patients?*

Sibyl. 'Nother second, 'nother second. *I was not lying!* 'Nother second—

Stephen Hastings. Because you had no choice?

Asa. That's it, Charlotte. He's comin' now. He's—

> *(CHARLOTTE'S chin shoots up. She lets out a slight squeal.)*

Anne. I saw her eyes roll up, then close.

Asa. I felt her body grow limp.

Sibyl. Then she lost consciousness.

Asa. Dear God.

Sibyl. Charlotte, wake up. Charlotte.

Anne. What happened?

Sibyl. Go get a cool cloth. . . . Charlotte!

Asa. What's wrong?

Sibyl. She may have fainted.

Asa. Why would she—

Sibyl. Quiet. *(Checks CHARLOTTE'S breath.)* Anne!

Asa. What is it?

Anne. *(Returning.)* What?

Sibyl. Check her pulse. She's not breathing.

Anne. What happened?

Sibyl. We don't know. *(SIBYL clears CHARLOTTE'S tongue, tilts her head, preparing for mouth-to-mouth.)*

Asa. What do you think?

Sibyl. It could be a stroke. Try the phone again.

Asa. Still dead.

> *(SIBYL breathes twice into CHAR-LOTTE.)*

ANNE. Nothing here.

ASA. "Our Father, who art in heaven . . ." *(ASA prays throughout. SIBYL begins pushing down hard on CHARLOTTE'S chest with the heels of her hands.)*

SIBYL. ONE and TWO and THREE and FOUR and FIVE and SIX and SEVEN and EIGHT and NINE and TEN and ELEVEN and TWELVE and THIRTEEN and FOURTEEN and FIFTEEN! *(She resumes mouth-to-mouth.)*

TANNER. *You believed she had suffered a stroke, is that right?*

SIBYL. *(Between breaths.)* Yes.

TANNER. *A ruptured cerebral aneurysm, is that correct?*

SIBYL. Yes.

TANNER. *And why did you believe that?*

SIBYL. *(Resumes pumping on CHARLOTTE'S chest.)* ONE and TWO and THREE and—

TANNER. *Mrs. Danforth?*

SIBYL. FOUR and FIVE and SIX—

TANNER. *Why did you believe that a cerebral aneurysm had occurred?*

SIBYL. *(Still pumping.)* And NINE and TEN and *PUSHING.*

TANNER. *The pushing?*

SIBYL. And FOURTEEN and *YES!*

TANNER. *You believed that the pressure of Charlotte's exertions had caused a vessel in that poor woman's brain to burst, is that right?*

SIBYL. Anything? *(ANNE shakes her head. SIBYL resumes mouth-to-mouth.)*

TANNER. *You believed that the hours and hours of torture you had put that woman through had finally killed her.*

SIBYL. No.

TANNER. *You believed you had murdered Charlotte Bedford.*

SIBYL. NO! and TWO and THREE and you CAN and you CAN and you CAN you CAN and PLEASE and PLEASE and PLEASE . . .

CONNIE. *(Overlapping.)* And NINE and TEN and ELEVEN and TWELVE and THIRTEEN and FOURTEEN and FIFTEEN! . . .

> *(ALL look at ANNE, who shakes her head.)*

SIBYL. Get me the sharpest knife in the house.

> *(ASA and ANNE begin to exit, stop.)*

ASA. *I thought she was going to use it to somehow save Charlotte. A tracheotomy or— She was in charge.*

ANNE. *Because I couldn't stand to be in the room with a dead woman.*

CONNIE. At another time, Anne claimed that she left the room because she was afraid of you. You seemed insane to her.

SIBYL. I was upset, yes, but I was not hysterical.

STEPHEN HASTINGS. *During the time that Asa and Miss Austin were out of the room, did you check one last time to see if the woman had a pulse?*

SIBYL. Yes.

STEPHEN HASTINGS. *Did you hear one?*

SIBYL. No.

STEPHEN HASTINGS. *Did you check one last time to see if she had a heartbeat?*

SIBYL. *Yes, absolutely.*

STEPHEN HASTINGS. *And did you hear one?*

SIBYL. *No, I did not.*

STEPHEN HASTINGS. *You did everything possible to make sure the woman was dead?*

    (ASA and ANNE return.)

SIBYL. I can't get a pulse, Asa.

ASA. Can't you do more CPR?

SIBYL. God, Asa, I could do it for days. She's not coming back.

ASA. . . . Charlotte. . . . Charlotte, I love you . . . Come back, please. Dear Lord, help me understand.

SIBYL. Let's go. We've got no time.

ASA. What do you mean?

SIBYL. The baby's only got a few moments, and we used most of them on Charlotte.

ASA. What are you going to do?

SIBYL. *(Picking up the knife.)* Save your baby. *(Pause. ASA nods.)*

TANNER. *Did she ask what you wanted to do?*

ASA. *No. She did not.*

TANNER. *Did she place the fetalscope back on Charlotte's stomach to check for the child's heartbeat?*

ANNE. *No. She did not.*

TANNER. *And did she, Reverend Bedford, check one last time to see if Charlotte had a pulse or a heartbeat, before she plunged a kitchen knife into your wife's abdomen?*

ASA & SIBYL. *She did not.*

CONNIE. Moments later, you reached into Charlotte's body,

and pulled from her . . . a boy. He was limp and pale, you had to work him hard. You sucked the mucus from his throat, you rubbed his back and hit the bottoms of his feet. You talked to him. You tried to get Asa to talk to him. And then he gasped, and he howled, and you handed him to his father. You had saved that little boy.

> *(ASA and ANNE roll the bed carrying CHARLOTTE off stage. SIBYL has returned to her IV.)*

SIBYL. Inside, I had to use my fingers. It was too close to the baby for a knife, so I slipped a finger into the uterus and just tore it open like it was pastry dough. . . . Did I ever tell you that? It was like damp pastry dough.

LOUISE. *(Entering.)* How's it going in here, ya doin' all right?

SIBYL. Fine.

LOUISE. What can I get ya? We got apple juice, orange—

SIBYL. I'm fine.

LOUISE. Stomach okay?

SIBYL. So far.

LOUISE. Connie? . . . You a look a little nauseous yourself. Sibyl, has she been stealing hits off your IV drip? These doctors and their prescription drug habits. . . . Seriously, you want some juice or something? I've got some warm seltzer I just put in the fridge.

CONNIE. I'm all set, thanks.

LOUISE. You don't take advantage of my hospitality I might turn on you.

CONNIE. Could I have a warm seltzer please?

SIBYL. Me too.

LOUISE. Two seltzers, comin' up. *(To SIBYL.)* She comes near that drip, you give her one these [a smack]. *(LOUISE exits.)*

SIBYL. Her body was too big to wrap in a blanket, so I sewed it up the best I could. Did you know that? I went to my bag and I got out my catgut. My tweezers. My curved needle.

CONNIE. Mom.

SIBYL. It took three packages of dissolvable sutures. Did you know that?

CONNIE. Stop.

SIBYL. Then you don't know everything, do you? You know what they told you, in court. That doesn't mean you know. You don't know my side.

CONNIE. Mom, this isn't about sides.

SIBYL. Of course it is. That's what a trial is.

CONNIE. This isn't a trial. Mom, listen. I know what happened because it was everywhere, okay? It was everything. It was the papers, the news, the mail. It was—

> *(An answering machine beeps. CONNIE, now 14, and SIBYL listen to a series of messages.)*

MAGGIE. Good morning, my name is Maggie Bressor, I'm a writer with the *Herald*. I would like to speak with Mrs. Sibyl Danforth as soon as she returns please.

MOLLY. Hi, Sibyl. Molly here. I heard about the . . . tragedy and, I'm thinking of you. I'm here. Call me when you feel up to it.

JOE. Hello, I'm looking for Sibyl Danforth. This is Joe Meehan with the *Sentinel*.

RITA. Sibyl? Are you there? If you're there but not picking up, please pick up. It's Rita. I have a whole file of legal stuff from the Midwives' Alliance of North America. It's huge. Okay, you're not there, I believe you.

CONNIE. Mom, why don't we just take it off the hook?

SIBYL. I'm waiting for a call.

CONNIE. From who?

SIBYL. Anne. . . . My apprentice.

CONNIE. Oh.

SIBYL. I left her a message. Last night. *(Phone rings. SIBYL starts to answer. Stops. They wait.)*

TIMOTHY. Timothy Stark with the Associated Press. Thought I'd try again.

SIBYL. You look at those paper clippings now and you think, maybe we should have been talking to the press. The other side certainly was.

DR. DUMMOND. *(To an INTERVIEWER.)* We've all been lulled into believing that birth is as safe as having a cavity filled or a broken arm set. Obviously, as this incident proves, it's not. The list of things that can go wrong in a home birth is frightening and it is endless.

TANNER. *(To an INTERVIEWER.)* We won't know for a while whether there's a basis for criminal charges, or whether it's merely a civil matter.

DR. DUMMOND. At this point I have no idea whether the woman would have died in a hospital. I don't know the details of what happened. But would she have had her stomach ripped open with a kitchen knife? Of course not. Would she have had to endure a cesarean section without anesthesia? Of course not.

ASA. *(To an INTERVIEWER.)* I am very, very grateful that I have been blessed with another child. But I don't even know how to begin to convey my grief over Charlotte's death. I'm sorry, I shouldn't say anymore.

SIBYL. You see, that's my point. Everything you heard, everything you read was secondhand. Even the good news, like Stephen Hastings.

> *(Cut to court scene. Note: From this point on, courtroom excerpts will no longer be distinguished by italics.)*

STEPHEN HASTINGS. *(Addressing the JURY.)* I have in my hand the copy of a two-hundred-year-old diary by a woman named Priscilla Mayhew. Miss Mayhew was a midwife in Fullerton, New Hampshire, and like many midwives, she was probably viewed by the village with a mixture of awe and envy, fear and respect. That's how it's always been with midwives. To some people, they're witches— or, these days, strange and somehow dangerous throwbacks to another era. But in the eyes of other people, they're healers. Not surprisingly, it always seems to be the women who see them as healers, and the men who are quick to cry witch. Midwives, by their very nature and profession, have always challenged authority. The history of midwifery in America is filled with the names of women lionized by their own gender and ostracized

by men. Names like Anne Hutchinson. That's right, the
first female religious leader in Colonial America was also
a midwife. In addition to having a brilliant mind, Anne
Hutchinson had the strong heart and gentle hands of a
midwife. And she had her followers. So what happened
to Anne? The *men* of Massachusetts banished her to the
rough woods which, with her help, became the state of
Rhode Island. Did they ask the mothers how they felt
about this? Of course not. Now according to the records
Mrs. Mayhew kept in this diary, she witnessed one maternal death for every one hundred ninety-two happy,
healthy births. Is that an acceptable mortality rate by our
late-twentieth century standards? No? In this country today, barely one in ten thousand mothers die in childbirth. And yet as recently as fifty years ago in the United
States, one woman in one hundred and fifty died as a
result of childbirth. You can look it up at the National
Center for Health Statistics. Is there an irony here? You
bet. Fifty years ago in the United States most women
were laboring in hospitals, and they were laboring in the
care of physicians. In other words, Priscilla Mayhew,
eighteenth-century midwife, had a dramatically lower
mortality rate than physicians practicing as recently as
1930. And while obstetrics have made impressive leaps
in the last fifty years, the statistics show that today a
planned home birth is every bit as safe as a hospital birth.
Every bit as safe, for babies as well as mothers. Now as
you will see . . .

CONNIE. *(Hands STEPHEN HASTINGS a cup of coffee. He joins SIBYL at her kitchen table.)* Black, right?

STEPHEN HASTINGS. Perfect.

SIBYL. And you of course had a crush on him.

CONNIE. I did not!

SIBYL. *(To AUDIENCE.)* She did.

CONNIE. I just noticed that he always dressed better than the men around him.

SIBYL. So you asked him about it.

STEPHEN HASTINGS. Well, I figure that to win at what I do—and let's face it, charge what I charge—I need to look one click above the competition. Not two clicks, because then I look like an idiot. One. One makes me look pricey. And, I hope, worth it.

CONNIE. We hope so, too.

SIBYL. Connie!

STEPHEN HASTINGS. That's okay. She's looking out for your interests.

SIBYL. Well, right now she's heading upstairs to look out for her homework.

CONNIE. It's earth science, I can do it here.

SIBYL. Connie . . .

CONNIE. I'm going. . . . *(Turning back to SIBYL.)* But do you think I would have gone so easily, if it weren't for the floor grate in my bedroom? I spent half my fourteenth year with my ear pressed against that grate. There was nothing secondhand about what I heard you and Stephen discussing.

STEPHEN HASTINGS. *(To PHOTOGRAPHER.)* Let's start with the hands.

SIBYL. Stephen, I haven't been charged with anything yet.

STEPHEN HASTINGS. We're preparing for the worst.

SIBYL. And what's that?

STEPHEN HASTINGS. Well, with Tanner, I wouldn't be surprised if he starts making noise about it being intentional.

SIBYL. What does that mean?

PHOTOGRAPHER. Turn, please.

STEPHEN HASTINGS. In fact, it wouldn't mean anything. But as the State's top gun in this county, Tanner needs to be the big cowboy. If he suggests you acted intentionally, it means he thinks he can win a charge of voluntary manslaughter, not just involuntary. Maybe even second degree murder.

SIBYL. He thinks I not only killed Charlotte, I did it on purpose?

STEPHEN HASTINGS. We don't know. He may not bring any charges. If he does, though, I'd like the jury to see just how hard you tried to get that woman to the hospital.

SIBYL. If he doesn't, I'll have some lovely illustrations for my journal.

STEPHEN HASTINGS. You keep a journal?

SIBYL. Yes. Is that a problem?

CONNIE. When it wasn't Stephen, the house was full of pilgrims. *(A procession of MIDWIVES pass through.)* Midwives from all over New England and upstate New York started showing up to share their stories and console you.

Every time there was a knock, another casserole or stew would appear on our counter. Or bread. Fresh breads. Their poems appeared on the fridge. They flooded the editorial pages; they lobbied their legislators. I guess the doctors were off mobilizing for battle too, though. *(We see the backs of a group of men. They look at SIBYL, then turn away.)* Led by some very angry ob-gyns, they saw this case as their chance to slam the door on hippie women practicing medicine without a license.

SIBYL. Not all of them, though. Not my backup physician. *(A knock.)*

CONNIE. Mom, it's Dr. Hewitt.

SIBYL. Barton!

BARTON. You stay put. How's that ankle?

SIBYL. Which one?

BARTON. Geez, you really did it, huh?

SIBYL. I guess so. Will you have some pie, or do we have any of that banana bread left?

CONNIE. We have tons of everything.

BARTON. No. Thanks. I'm just on my way home.

SIBYL. Barton, this isn't on your way home.

BARTON. I had a little news . . .

CONNIE. I guess that's my cue to do dishes.

SIBYL. Thanks, sweetie. *(CONNIE exits. BARTON gestures to SIBYL'S ankles.)*

BARTON. You get those looked at yet?

SIBYL. Yes, no break.

BARTON. Don't think I've ever seen you with your feet up.

SIBYL. I overdid a little today.

BARTON. . . . Sibyl, I'm wondering if you've heard from Anne recently.

SIBYL. No. I've been trying to reach her for three days.

BARTON. I asked her to call you.

SIBYL. *(Calling off.)* Honey, did Anne call today? *(CONNIE, who is eavesdropping, clatters some plates together.)*

CONNIE. What?

SIBYL. Any word from Anne?

CONNIE. Nope.

SIBYL. Well, the phone's been pretty busy. Anyway I see her tomorrow, we've got a prenatal at ten.

BARTON. I don't think so, Sibyl.

SIBYL. What do you mean?

BARTON. How well do you know Anne?

SIBYL. Fairly well. She's been with me for almost three months now. . . . What?

BARTON. She called me. The morning after.

SIBYL. What for?

BARTON. When you made the incision, she says she saw blood spurt. A couple of times. She thinks Mrs. Bedford was alive. *(Pause. CONNIE scrapes a plate to break the silence.)*

SIBYL. If you'd like, I'll talk to Anne tomorrow and put an end to this.

BARTON. She won't be here tomorrow, Sibyl. That's what I'm telling you.

SIBYL. Is that why you're here?

BARTON. That's part of it. . . . I was interviewed today, by a couple of state troopers.

SIBYL. They talked to me too. They're trying to be thorough.

BARTON. Sibyl, listen, based on their questions, I got the distinct impression that everyone—State's Attorney, medical examiner, Anne Austin, the father—they all believe that someone is dead right now because you performed a bedroom cesarean on a living woman.

JUDGE DORSET. How do you plead?

SIBYL & CONNIE. Not guilty.

TANNER. A midwife is an outlaw, who by her very nature demonstrates a reckless disregard for authority, and for the established medical norms of our society. Sibyl Danforth has a long history of challenging the state, first as an anti-war protester and now as a midwife. Given that history, and given the fact that she is facing fifteen years in prison if convicted, the State believes there is a real and significant danger of flight.

STEPHEN HASTINGS. Your Honor, we all know there is no risk of flight. My client has lived in the same town almost her entire life.

TANNER. Moreover, she faces the loss of her practice—such as it is.

STEPHEN HASTINGS. And let's not forget she's the mother of a fourteen-year-old girl.

TANNER. She has no job, Your Honor, her career is in shambles, reputation irrevocably tarnished. The State would like to see bail set at thirty-five thousand dollars.

STEPHEN HASTINGS. That's absurd!

JUDGE DORSET. Gentlemen, a tragedy has brought us here today, and we are probably about to embark upon a long road together. I, for one, can do without such hyperbole as "outlaw" this early in the process. Mrs. Danforth, do you have any travel plans between now and the time of your trial?

SIBYL. No, Your Honor.

JUDGE DORSET. In that case, I see no reason to impose a monetary condition for release. Let's move on.

TANNER. *(To an imagined PROSPECTIVE JUROR.)* Do you have any children, Mr. Goodyear? . . . How old are they? . . . Are you married? . . . What does your wife do? . . . Grow up around here, did you? . . . Lucky man. One of the most beautiful parts of the state. Where were you born? . . . Right here. Good for you. In a hospital? . . . How about your boys, were they born in a hospital too? . . . Were the labors easy? Hard? In between? . . . Well, for your wife then. . . . Did you two ever consider having your boys at home? . . . And why not?

STEPHEN HASTINGS. Miss Rice, who has the burden of proof? . . . Well, it's a legal term. We have two sides in this courtroom; I represent the defense and Mr. Tanner over there, represents the State. One of us will have to prove something inside these walls over the next few weeks and one of us won't. Am I the one who has to prove something? . . . And what would that be? . . . Mr. Anderson, do you agree with Miss Rice that I have to prove something in these proceedings? . . . And why is that? . . . Thank you, Mr. Anderson, don't go anywhere, we'll talk more in a moment. Miss Rice, what do you think of what Mr. Anderson just said? . . . About whether I have to prove my client is innocent. . . . Actually it's not just Mr. Anderson, it's our entire system of jurisprudence. If you're a juror, you need to begin with the presumption that my client is innocent. Can you do that? . . . What aren't you sure about? . . . Your Honor, may I approach the bench?

JUDGE DORSET. That won't be necessary. Miss Rice, the court thanks you for your willingness to spend the day with us. You are excused.

>   *(SIBYL is writing in the journal.*
>   *CONNIE approaches, holding a mug*
>   *of tea.)*

CONNIE. Kettle's hot.

SIBYL. Hmm?

CONNIE. There's hot water, if you want.

SIBYL. I'm all set. You heading upstairs?

CONNIE. Yeah, I'm dead.

SIBYL. All that excitement in court today?

CONNIE. It's not that bad.

SIBYL. Probably makes you want to be a lawyer when you grow up.

CONNIE. Or a midwife.

SIBYL. I'll bet. . . . You were quiet tonight. You okay?

CONNIE. Yeah, I'm just . . .

SIBYL. What? Come here. . . . Come sit on your mother's lap.

CONNIE. I'd crush you.

SIBYL. Sit.

CONNIE. Am I too much?

SIBYL. Go ahead. I won't break.

CONNIE. What are you writing?

SIBYL. "Confessions of a Mad Midwife." Now . . . what is it?

CONNIE. I'm just tired.

SIBYL. You know, you don't have to go tomorrow . . .

CONNIE. No, I do. I just— I didn't know Mrs. Bedford's sister would be there.

SIBYL. I know. It's very . . .

CONNIE. The way she looks at us.

SIBYL. At me.

CONNIE. No, it's both of us. She knows who I am. And she's so full of— She's so sure that we killed her sister. That we're liars. How can she think that?

SIBYL. Well, people can have different versions of an event without being liars. I even have different versions from myself. I remember something one way, and then later, I start to see it differently. Doesn't mean I'm lying. And it matters who's asking. There are things I'd tell Stephen that I would never say in court. And there are things I would tell you, if you wanted to know . . .

CONNIE. Like what?

SIBYL. About that night. What happened.

CONNIE. I know what happened, because I know you.

SIBYL. Well, good, because my leg is about to break off.

CONNIE. I told you I'm too big.

SIBYL. Oo. Ow. Ow. Ow. I think I *will* warm this tea up a little. Should I bring the kettle?

CONNIE. Nah, I'm just going to bed.

SIBYL. See you in the morning then. . . . Don't forget your mug. *(SIBYL exits. CONNIE returns for the mug. She looks down at the open journal. The sound of FREEZING RAIN against a window. She sees CHARLOTTE in the half-light, staring back at her. CONNIE picks up the journal and reads. We hear the voice of SIBYL.)* "I could probably figure out roughly the number of times I've reread what I wrote on March 15. I'd just have to count on the calendar the number of days since then to get a good estimate, because few days have gone by when I haven't looked at that entry. It's like a car accident to me. I'm drawn to it. I find myself staring at the words. . . . Next week I'm going to sit on the witness stand, I'm going to tell everyone what I think happened, and I'll probably find it in me to be cool and together about it. I'm sure I'll be as confident about what happened as Stephen wants me to be, because that's what I have to do now, for me, and for Connie. But the truth of the matter is, I just don't have any idea anymore what really happened." *(CONNIE turns back the pages. She locates another entry.)* "March 15, 1981 . . ."

END ACT ONE

ACT II

(Hospital. CONNIE and SIBYL sit silently.)

SIBYL. *(To AUDIENCE.)* Transition. Those moments between the first and second stage when the opening process is complete and the will to go forward is absent. She teeters there, pure emotion. Her rational mind has left. She needs yours. She needs you to know exactly where she's at and talk exactly to that state of consciousness. Come on preachy and she'll ignore you. If she's afraid, she needs your humor. If you're afraid, she'll see through you. She'll know you're a fraud, and then you've lost her.

LOUISE. *(Entering.)* Two very slightly chilled seltzers.

SIBYL. Thank you.

LOUISE. I got sidetracked out there. Otherwise they'd still be warm. *(Checking the IV.)* Looks like we're getting down to the dregs here.

SIBYL. I was thirsty.

CONNIE. About how much longer?

LOUISE. What your mother's paying for this room, she should stay and get her money's worth. . . . We've got another thirty-five minutes, then we'll let you catch your breath and off you go. . . . You're gonna tell me if you start feeling dizzy, right?

SIBYL. So far, so good.

LOUISE. I will return. *(To CONNIE.)* You know, a lot of

people try to cheer things up when they visit. Happy thoughts. Good old days. That sort of thing.

SIBYL. I think Louise is saying we should look through this [the journal].

LOUISE. You got pictures? Pictures are perfect.

CONNIE. It's a journal.

LOUISE. Better still. Who wants to look at herself when she was younger and prettier? Sit down with your mother and reminisce.

SIBYL. She'll turn on you . . .

LOUISE. If you got anything about Connie in there, might be humiliating . . . wait 'til I get back, okay? *(LOUISE exits. SIBYL thumbs through.)*

CONNIE. You are relentless.

SIBYL. Happy thoughts . . .

CONNIE. Look, I didn't come here to— I don't want to go backward.

SIBYL. We don't have much forward left.

CONNIE. Mom, I don't know if this is what you need to hear, but this is the truth, okay? You . . . are my hero. I don't know any woman or man with your courage, or your integrity, or your ability to think the best of people. Even dirtballs. *(They hug.)* You are still my hero, Mom, okay? No matter what happened. *(SIBYL recoils.)* What?

SIBYL. Nothing. *(To AUDIENCE.)* Have you ever waited for bad news so long, that when it finally comes . . . *(To CONNIE.)* Thank you.

CONNIE. What are you talking about?

SIBYL. Thank you for finally admitting what's wrong between us.

CONNIE. Nothing's wrong.

SIBYL. Connie, please. You think I killed her. You're entitled—

CONNIE. Of course I don't.

SIBYL. It makes sense.

CONNIE. I don't think that. Mom—

SIBYL. Month after month, the news. The constant— Like you said, it was everywhere.

CONNIE. Stop. This is ridiculous.

SIBYL. And then the trial. How could anyone sit through that trial and not—

CONNIE. Mom, stop! . . . I really mean stop. We're not even going to talk for a minute. We're going to . . . we're going to have a drink. Have a drink. *(They drink.)*

SIBYL. Sweetie, I don't blame—

CONNIE. No!

SIBYL. . . . Do I have to have another drink? *(Toasting AUDI-ENCE.)* Welcome to the second stage.

CONNIE. They used to burn midwives, Mom, did you know that? They'd burn 'em for bad outcomes, they'd burn 'em for good ones. They didn't want anyone fiddling with God's plan, which had a convenient way of being their plan. . . . What happened to you was not a trial, it was an assault. On midwifery. On alternative health care. On women.

TANNER. The defense is going to try to convince you that this is a complicated case, with a lot of gray in it. They are going to parade into this courtroom a lot of so-called experts who have probably never set foot in this state before. But you will soon see that this case isn't so complicated. You will see that from the moment Charlotte and Asa sat down with Sibyl Danforth to discuss having their baby at home, Mrs. Danforth behaved with the sort of gross irresponsibility that could only end in tragedy. Should Charlotte Bedford have been allowed to have that baby in her bedroom in the first place? You will see that other midwives—as well as every single reasonable physician on this planet—would have said no. The risk was too great. On the day that Charlotte Bedford went into labor, did Sibyl Danforth even demonstrate the common sense to consider the weather? A woman born and raised right here, who well knows the vicissitudes of our weather? She did not. And on that night, when she realized that because of her own astonishing lack of foresight she and a woman in labor were cornered in a bedroom miles and miles from the help that a hospital would have provided, what did she do? She had Charlotte push . . . and push . . . and push. Hours beyond what a healthy woman could have endured, she had her push. Without anesthesia. Without painkillers. Sibyl Danforth had that woman push for so long that she thought she had killed her. The irony? Sibyl Danforth hadn't pushed her to death. She almost had. But not quite. Charlotte Bedford did not die from pushing. It took a ten-inch knife with a six-inch blade to do that.

(CONNIE watches as CHARLOTTE takes her seat in court. CONNIE remains aware of CHARLOTTE throughout the trial.)

SIBYL. (*To AUDIENCE.*) I think we're now fully engaged.

TANNER. Miss Martin, how long have you been a certified nurse-midwife?

MISS MARTIN. Fourteen years.

TANNER. Would you tell us what it means to be a certified nurse-midwife?

MISS MARTIN. First of all, we're all registered nurses. We have formal medical training. Secondly, we've all graduated from one of two dozen advanced-education programs around the country that focus on women's health care and midwifery. Third, we've all passed the certification exam given by the American College of Nurse-Midwives. Finally—and I believe this is very important—we all meet the requirements of the health agencies or medical boards of the state where we practice.

TANNER. Do you have any other training in this area?

MISS MARTIN. Yes, I have a masters degree. From Marquette.

TANNER. Are you a member of the American College of Nurse-Midwives?

MISS MARTIN. I am. I am also part of the Division of Accreditation.

TANNER. I see. Miss Martin, how many nurse-midwives are there in this country?

MISS MARTIN. About twenty-five thousand.

TANNER. Do most nurse-midwives deliver babies at home?

MISS MARTIN. No. The vast majority of us work in hospitals or birthing centers. Almost ninety-five percent of us.

TANNER. What about you?

MISS MARTIN. I have delivered babies at home, but I was much younger then.

TANNER. Why did you stop delivering babies at home?

MISS MARTIN. In my opinion, it's a needless risk.

TANNER. And what changed your mind?

MISS MARTIN. Education. The more I learned about obstetrics, the more I realized that home birth exposes everyone—mother and infant—to completely unnecessary hazards. Especially now, with the advent of birthing centers which are designed to create a home-like atmosphere.

TANNER. Thank you.

STEPHEN HASTINGS. Miss Martin, you said that roughly ninety-five percent of nurse-midwives work in hospitals and birthing centers. Does that mean roughly five percent don't?

MISS MARTIN. Yes.

STEPHEN HASTINGS. That five percent, do they work in homes?

MISS MARTIN. Yes.

STEPHEN HASTINGS. Do they have a higher infant mortality rate than the rest of the group?

MISS MARTIN. The numbers are small, so it's hard to make a statistical comparison.

STEPHEN HASTINGS. Bearing that in mind, is there a higher infant mortality rate in home births?

Miss Martin. No.

Stephen Hastings. How about maternal mortality? Do you see a greater incidence of maternal mortality among midwives delivering babies at home?

Miss Martin. No.

Stephen Hastings. In fact, did any nurse-midwife in your organization see a woman die in home birth last year?

Miss Martin. I don't think so. But that doesn't diminish—

Stephen Hastings. In fact, none died. Miss Martin, you testified that you sit on the Division of Accreditation, is that right?

Miss Martin. Yes.

Stephen Hastings. I assume from your testimony that you do not sit on the Home Birth Committee, am I right?

Miss Martin. That's right.

Stephen Hastings. But there is such a committee?

Miss Martin. Yes.

Stephen Hastings. So there are other members of the American College of Nurse-Midwives—registered nurses, with formal medical training, graduates of advanced-education programs, who have passed your certification exam, who meet the requirements of the health agencies and medical boards of their states, who have in fact been accredited by the board on which you serve—there are other members of your organization who disagree with your position on home birth, is that right?

Miss Martin. It appears that way, yes.

Connie. The next witness? Another midwife who'd decided

"home birth wasn't such a good idea," only this one became an ob-gyn.

SIByL. Dr. Gerson? I thought she was very impressive.

CONNIE. That was the *idea*. Two books on prenatal care, faculty member at the B.U. School of Medicine.

SIByL. They're *supposed* to be experts, dear. I wonder if she's still there. You'll have to tell me.

STEPHEN HASTINGS. Are many pregnant women anemic?

DR. GERSON. I wouldn't say "anemic," but many experience a small degree of anemia.

STEPHEN HASTINGS. Is it treatable?

DR. GERSON. Yes.

STEPHEN HASTINGS. How?

DR. GERSON. Iron tablets. Ferrous sulfate, usually.

STEPHEN HASTINGS. You said you reviewed how Sibyl treated Charlotte Bedford's anemia, correct?

DR. GERSON. That's right.

STEPHEN HASTINGS. What did Sibyl do?

DR. GERSON. She had her take iron tablets.

STEPHEN HASTINGS. Ferrous sulfate?

DR. GERSON. Yes.

STEPHEN HASTINGS. Did her condition improve?

DR. GERSON. Not enough to merit—

STEPHEN HASTINGS. Did Charlotte Bedford's condition improve?

DR. GERSON. Yes.

STEPHEN HASTINGS. Dr. Gerson, do you recognize these?

DR. GERSON. They're the records your midwife kept of the deceased.

STEPHEN HASTINGS. The records you reviewed?

DR. GERSON. Part of them, yes.

STEPHEN HASTINGS. I want to focus on the hemocrit values, the percentage of blood occupied by red corpuscles. According to this, what was Charlotte Bedford's hemocrit value in September?

DR. GERSON. Thirty-one percent.

STEPHEN HASTINGS. How about February?

DR. GERSON. Thirty-five percent.

STEPHEN HASTINGS. Is that an improvement?

DR. GERSON. A slight one.

STEPHEN HASTINGS. Dr. Gerson, when one of your patients has a hemocrit value of thirty-five percent, do you anticipate a bad outcome?

DR. GERSON. I don't see how that's relevant. I deliver babies in hospitals. If you mean, would it—

STEPHEN HASTINGS. I'll repeat the question: Would you anticipate a bad outcome?

DR. GERSON. No.

STEPHEN HASTINGS. Thank you.

DR. GERSON. You're welcome.

STEPHEN HASTINGS. Dr. Gerson, is there any indication in Charlotte Bedford's medical history that she had been treated for hypertension?

DR. GERSON. I didn't see any.

STEPHEN HASTINGS. Am I correct that there's a box on the form in front of you that says, "Patient's History"?

DR. GERSON. Yes, there is.

STEPHEN HASTINGS. And what has been circled in the box?

DR. GERSON. Bladder infections. German measles.

STEPHEN HASTINGS. Have the words "high blood pressure" been circled?

DR. GERSON. No.

STEPHEN HASTINGS. In fact, there is no indication that Charlotte Bedford shared her history of high blood pressure with Sibyl, is there, Doctor?

DR. GERSON. Counsel, these records show the poor woman had symptoms of both anemia and high blood pressure. No doctor or midwife in her right mind would have allowed that poor woman to labor at home.

STEPHEN HASTINGS. Your Honor!

JUDGE DORSET. The witness's last remark will be struck from the record.

CONNIE. Right. And the jurors are going to strike those comments from their memories. Who can do that?

SIBYL. Not you, I guess.

CONNIE. Because it's so unfair! People could get up there and say anything.

DR. LANG. It's perfectly reasonable that someone with the limited training of a midwife would suspect a ruptured cerebral aneurysm.

CONNIE. Limited training.

DR. LANG. Obviously that's not what occurred in this case, but someone with only rudimentary obstetric education might think such a thing.

CONNIE. Rudimentary obstetric— And people had to listen to this.

TANNER. In your opinion, Dr. Lang, what did occur?

DR. LANG. She *vagaled*. It's a shorthand term we doctors tend to use, but clearly that's what happened. She vagaled out.

CONNIE. Those were just the rehearsed assaults. Then there were the "accidental" ones. Little Anne Austin, unable to contain herself.

SIBYL. Remember what we used to call her? Anne Austin, Anne Austin, all the way from Boston.

CONNIE. Before the trial, yeah.

STEPHEN HASTINGS. Prior to March 14, 1981, you had only seen nine births, correct?

ANNE. Yes.

STEPHEN HASTINGS. And none of them resulted in an emergency situation, right?

ANNE. That's right.

STEPHEN HASTINGS. Had you ever been in a life and death situation?

ANNE. No.

STEPHEN HASTINGS. Had you ever been with an EMT or rescue squad during an emergency?

ANNE. No.

STEPHEN HASTINGS. Charlotte Bedford was the first, wasn't she?

ANNE. Yes, she was.

STEPHEN HASTINGS. Do you have any formal medical training?

ANNE. Not yet, but I'm planning on—

STEPHEN HASTINGS. Thank you, Miss Austin. Let me see, perhaps you've taken an accredited first-aid course, have you?

ANNE. No.

STEPHEN HASTINGS. When you saw the blood that resulted from Sibyl's attempt to save the baby, was that the first time you'd ever seen a body opened?

ANNE. I guess.

STEPHEN HASTINGS. Yes?

ANNE. Yes.

STEPHEN HASTINGS. So prior to the early morning hours of March 14th, you had never seen the quantities of blood that might or might not flow in that situation, correct?

ANNE. Yes.

STEPHEN HASTINGS. You'd never seen blood spurt from a living or a dead body?

ANNE. No.

STEPHEN HASTINGS. In that case, Miss Austin, what in your background led you to assume that the blood you saw that morning was coming from a living woman?

ANNE. It was the way it spurted.

STEPHEN HASTINGS. No, let me clarify. I'm not asking you what you think you saw. I'm asking what in your background led you to conclude that based on the bleeding Charlotte Bedford was alive?

ANNE. You didn't see it. If you had been—

STEPHEN HASTINGS. Your Honor, please instruct the witness.

JUDGE DORSET. Miss Austin, you will answer the question.

ANNE. But if any of—

JUDGE DORSET. Miss Austin, answer the questions as they are asked. Please. Mr. Hastings, proceed.

STEPHEN HASTINGS. What part of your training led you to think that the blood you saw was coming from a living person?

ANNE. I don't recall.

STEPHEN HASTINGS. Is that because you have none—absolutely no medical training?

ANNE. I guess.

STEPHEN HASTINGS. Am I correct in saying that any conjectures you made about the blood were founded on absolutely no experience—no first- or second- or even third-hand experience?

ANNE. God, Sibyl, I'm sorry, but I had to do it, I had to call! You know you killed her. You know—

STEPHEN HASTINGS. Your Honor! I demand that these comments be struck from the record.

JUDGE DORSET. *(Pounding his gavel.)* Miss Austin.

ANNE. I'm sorry, Sibyl, I am! I know you didn't mean to, but we both know you killed her!

JUDGE DORSET. Miss Austin!

STEPHEN HASTINGS. *(While JUDGE DORSET quiets the court.)* She is a little witch, isn't she?

SIBYL. No. She isn't really. She's just young.

STEPHEN HASTINGS. That's big of you.

SIBYL. I think she just got herself in too deep.

STEPHEN HASTINGS. Well then, she's about to drown. We're about to take Miss Austin down for the third time.

JUDGE DORSET. Miss Austin, you will focus solely on the question Mr. Hastings is asking, and Mr. Hastings, you will allow the witness to answer each question fully. Do we have an understanding?

STEPHEN HASTINGS. Can we please have the court reporter read back the last question?

COURT REPORTER. Am I correct in saying that any conjectures you made about the blood were founded on absolutely no experience—no first- or second- or even third-hand experience?

ANNE. That's right.

STEPHEN HASTINGS. Nevertheless, when Sibyl made the first incision, you decided Charlotte Bedford was still alive.

ANNE. When I saw the blood, yes.

STEPHEN HASTINGS. Did the body show any other signs of life as the incision was made—or for that matter, after?

ANNE. Like what?

STEPHEN HASTINGS. Did the woman cry out with pain?

ANNE. She was unconscious.

STEPHEN HASTINGS. Did the body . . . flinch?

ANNE. I didn't see that.

STEPHEN HASTINGS. You didn't see it flinch. Did it move at all?

ANNE. Not that I saw.

STEPHEN HASTINGS. So the only indication you had that the woman was alive was the blood?

ANNE. Yes.

STEPHEN HASTINGS. And what did you do at that point? Did you try to stop Sibyl from proceeding?

ANNE. No.

STEPHEN HASTINGS. Did you say, "Don't do this Sibyl, she's alive?"

ANNE. No.

STEPHEN HASTINGS. Did you try to take the knife from Sibyl's hand?

TANNER. Objection. This is just badgering.

JUDGE DORSET. Overruled.

STEPHEN HASTINGS. Did you try to take the knife from Sibyl's hand?

ANNE. No.

STEPHEN HASTINGS. Did you share your fear with the father while the two of you were in the room?

ANNE. Not then I didn't.

STEPHEN HASTINGS. You testified earlier that you were surprised Sibyl never checked for a fetal heartbeat. Did you suggest that perhaps she should?

ANNE. No.

STEPHEN HASTINGS. So am I correct in saying that despite your claim, after the fact, that Charlotte Bedford had been alive before the incision, you did absolutely nothing to try and prevent the surgery?

ANNE. I just didn't know what—

STEPHEN HASTINGS. Miss Austin—

ANNE. I didn't know what to—

STEPHEN HASTINGS. Your Honor— *(The GAVEL sounds.)*

CONNIE. Stephen was ready to finish her, and what does Judge Dorset do? He throws her a life preserver.

JUDGE DORSET. Counsel. You agreed to allow the witness to

answer each question fully. Go ahead, Miss Austin.

ANNE. . . . I just didn't have the confidence at the time to stop her. Like you said, I hadn't been through anything like that. But I saw the blood pumping and pumping and I knew that was wrong, and it was only a few hours later that I decided I had a, a moral responsibility to tell someone. . . . I didn't want to. But I knew I had to.

CONNIE. Of course, Tanner had timed it perfectly to end the first week with Tierney, the State's medical examiner. That way we'd have the whole weekend to let those gruesome images burn in, before his grand finale on Monday.

TANNER. Mr. Tierney, when you arrived did Mrs. Danforth tell you how Charlotte Bedford had died?

TIERNEY. She said the lady had a stroke.

TANNER. What did you think?

TIERNEY. I thought it was possible. Anything's possible in a home birth.

STEPHEN HASTINGS. Objection!

JUDGE DORSET. Sustained.

TANNER. When you conducted the autopsy, did you find any indication that the woman had suffered a stroke?

TIERNEY. No.

TANNER. If there had been a stroke, would you have been able to detect it?

TIERNEY. Definitely. Absolutely.

TANNER. Did you also inspect Charlotte Bedford's abdominal area?

TIERNEY. We inspect everything.

TANNER. Could you tell where in the birth canal the baby had been when Mrs. Danforth removed it?

TIERNEY. No.

TANNER. Could you tell if the baby had descended at all during those hours when Mrs. Danforth forced Charlotte to push?

STEPHEN HASTINGS. Objection, no one forced anyone to do anything.

JUDGE DORSET. Sustained.

TIERNEY. No, I couldn't tell.

TANNER. Could you tell if there had been a placental abruption?

TIERNEY. Yes, definitely. There were areas of hemorrhage.

TANNER. Was that the cause of death?

TIERNEY. No. But it was a contributing factor.

TANNER. How so?

TIERNEY. Well, as any mother knows, labor's hard work. A woman needs all the strength she can muster, especially if something . . . unforeseen occurs.

TANNER. Did something unforeseen occur in this case?

TIERNEY. Other than the woman dying?

TANNER. Yes.

TIERNEY. Well, yes.

TANNER. Based on your autopsy, and the subsequent laboratory work, what do you think that something was?

TIERNEY. Well, we know there was no stroke, but that all the eyewitnesses saw something that looked like one. The woman spasmed and then blacked out. They all saw it.

But I don't believe it was an aneurysm that caused the spasm.

TANNER. Do you have an opinion as to its cause?

TIERNEY. Yes, in fact I do. To use Dr. Lang's expression, I believe the woman "vagaled."

TANNER. Would you elaborate?

TIERNEY. Right here in the back of our heads, there is a pair of cranial nerves filled with motor and sensory fibers. The vagus nerves. They communicate between the brain and the heart. They tell the heart how fast to beat. Now, like everything else in the body, the brain needs oxygen, which is carried to it in the blood—blood pumped, of course, by the heart. It's a circular system and when something goes wrong and the brain stops getting enough oxygen—if it goes what we call hypoxic—the brain stops functioning properly. Or at all. Obviously, there are a lot of things that can cause a brain to go hypoxic, including a planned medical event like anesthesia. But another cause may be labor. You take in those very deep breaths, work very hard, then exhale all at once. If someone does this hour after hour, they may suddenly go hypoxic.

TANNER. Is this dangerous?

TIERNEY. Absolutely. The heart can slow, or even stop. It's a reflex mediated by the vagus nerve. Your heart stops and you pass out. As some doctors say, you "vagal" out.

TANNER. Can it be fatal?

TIERNEY. Oh yes. But almost never for a woman in labor, because a delivery room nurse or ob-gyn knows exactly what the early symptoms look like, and it's easy to treat.

You have the woman relax or—in an extreme case—you just administer oxygen.

TANNER. In your opinion Charlotte Bedford vagaled. Was that the cause of death?

TIERNEY. Well, that's the thing, I don't think so. I believe the CPR Mrs. Danforth performed actually brought the woman back.

TANNER. What makes you think so?

TIERNEY. The amount of blood in the peritoneal cavity—the abdomen. There were close to a thousand milliliters in there. Plus all the blood outside the wound. Around the incision. On the bedding. In my opinion, there would not have been that much blood if the woman had been dead when Mrs. Danforth performed the cesarean section.

TANNER. In that case, what was the cause of death?

TIERNEY. As I typed on the death certificate, she died of hemorrhagic shock caused by a cesarean section.

STEPHEN HASTINGS. Mr. Tierney, you testified that Mrs. Bedford had about a thousand milliliters of blood in her abdomen. Am I correct?

TIERNEY. About that, yes.

STEPHEN HASTINGS. Under these circumstances, wouldn't you have expected more?

TIERNEY. A thousand is a good amount of blood.

STEPHEN HASTINGS. But if someone told you a woman had died from a C-section, wouldn't you have expected to find more than that?

TIERNEY. . . . I might have.

STEPHEN HASTINGS. If you wanted categorical, indisputable proof that a cesarean section had been the cause of death, how many milliliters of blood would you need to find in the abdominal cavity?

TIERNEY. Maybe . . . fifteen hundred.

STEPHEN HASTINGS. Was there that much blood in Charlotte Bedford's abdominal cavity?

TIERNEY. No.

STEPHEN HASTINGS. Thank you.

TANNER. One quick question, Dr. Tierney, if I may. . . . Given everything else you learned from the autopsy, and given the huge amount of blood found outside the abdominal cavity, was one thousand milliliters enough to convince you that the cesarean section performed by the defendant was the cause of death?

TIERNEY. Oh yes. Definitely.

TANNER. Thank you.

JUDGE DORSET. The court now stands adjourned. We will reconvene at ten o'clock, Monday morning.

STEPHEN HASTINGS. *(To SIBYL.)* I don't want you spending the weekend preoccupied with what the jury is thinking. There's still a very long way to go.

CONNIE. But you said our part would be short. Much shorter than theirs.

STEPHEN HASTINGS. It will be. All we need to do is plant reasonable doubt. That doesn't necessarily take long. . . . Connie? . . . We haven't had our turn yet, okay?

CONNIE. 'Kay.

STEPHEN HASTINGS. *(To SIBYL.)* Rest. Get your strength up. I'll come by Sunday to rehearse.

SIBYL. Are we doing a play?

STEPHEN HASTINGS. I want you ready.

SIBYL. You're not planning to grill me, are you?

STEPHEN HASTINGS. I'm saving that for the prosecution's last witness.

SIBYL. Stephen, you don't want to be too harsh, after all the poor man's been through.

STEPHEN HASTINGS. I'm not going to stand up there and bully the bereaved minister, if that's what you're worried about. It will be a careful dissection of his story. And they'll all be looking the wrong way when it comes to pieces.

SIBYL. But is it worth it? It's not like it's going to—

STEPHEN HASTINGS. Sibyl, I need you fired up. I need you ready for a fight, do you understand?

SIBYL. *(To AUDIENCE.)* Should I tell Connie what I wrote about that moment? That I was afraid. That I wanted to tell him, but I worried if I did, the floodgates would open and suddenly I'd be telling him that I was scared to go to jail, scared that I'd have to give up my practice. Should I tell her that, as I listened to all the testimony, I started to wonder, what if I did make a mistake back in March? What if that poor woman really was still alive?

TANNER. And so you asked Mrs. Danforth to try again?

ASA. I just couldn't believe Charlotte had really . . . passed away. I couldn't believe it. So yes, I think I said something like "Can't you do more CPR?"

TANNER. What did Mrs. Danforth tell you?

ASA. She said Charlotte was gone. She said she wasn't coming back.

TANNER. Did you believe her then?

ASA. Yes, sir, I did. It was like I had the wind knocked out of me and I remember I sort of sagged to the floor and, I laid my head on Charlotte's chest and I just stared up into her face. I told her I loved her. I told her I wanted her back. Then Mrs. Danforth said something like, "Let's move!" or "Let's go!" I had no idea what she meant. She sounded hysterical and—

STEPHEN HASTINGS. Objection.

JUDGE DORSET. Sustained.

TANNER. Reverend Bedford, what did Mrs. Danforth do next?

ASA. Well, she was wiping her eyes and . . . and flailing her arms. She kept saying, "We don't have any time, we don't have any time!" I asked her what she meant. She said we only had a few minutes to save the baby.

TANNER. Did she ask if you wanted her to try and save the baby?

ASA. No, sir.

TANNER. Before she began the cesarean section, did you see Mrs. Danforth check to see if Charlotte had a pulse?

ASA. No.

TANNER. Did you see her check to see if there was a heartbeat?

ASA. No.

TANNER. What about the baby? Did she check to see if the baby had a heartbeat?

ASA. No, sir, I did not see her do that.

TANNER. What did you do during the operation?

ASA. I . . . I went over to the window.

TANNER. Did you watch?

ASA. I watched some.

TANNER. Did you see the first incision?

ASA. Yes, sir.

TANNER. What do you remember about it—that first incision?

ASA. I remember blood . . . spurting. I remember seeing my Charlotte bleed.

STEPHEN HASTINGS. You asked if your wife was dead?

ASA. Yes, sir. And Mrs. Danforth said she was.

STEPHEN HASTINGS. What did you do next?

ASA. I didn't do anything.

STEPHEN HASTINGS. I believe, Reverend Bedford, we've already established that you went to the window. Am I mistaken?

ASA. No. That's right. I went to the window. . . . But then I looked back at Charlotte.

STEPHEN HASTINGS. From the window.

ASA. Yes, sir.

STEPHEN HASTINGS. *(Pointing to an easel or projection of the room in plan view.)* You were here?

ASA. That's right.

STEPHEN HASTINGS. Using the State's diagram and State's scale, you would have been approximately seven feet, nine inches from the center of the bed. Does that sound right to you?

ASA. It sounds . . . fine.

STEPHEN HASTINGS. Was it still night?

ASA. It was still dark, but it wasn't night. It was dark because of the storm. The clouds.

STEPHEN HASTINGS. And the only light in the room came from the lamps, here . . . and here. Is that correct?

ASA. Yes, but I could still see Charlotte.

STEPHEN HASTINGS. Where was Sibyl standing during the operation? On which side of the bed?

ASA. The far side.

STEPHEN HASTINGS. Here?

ASA. Yes.

STEPHEN HASTINGS. So this is Sibyl, and this is you. Correct?

ASA. Yes. I had an unobstructed view.

STEPHEN HASTINGS. Is this a bright light?

ASA. No. It's soft. Mrs. Danforth put in a special bulb to keep the lights low for the birth. But the other one was bright, the one she turned on before the . . . operation.

STEPHEN HASTINGS. How bright?

ASA. Very bright. It was our reading lamp.

STEPHEN HASTINGS. And where was the shadow?

ASA. What shadow?

STEPHEN HASTINGS. A lamp bright enough for reading will always cast a shadow, isn't that right?

ASA. I guess so.

STEPHEN HASTINGS. Where would the shadow have been?

ASA. On the bed.

STEPHEN HASTINGS. And, according to this diagram, where exactly on the bed would that shadow have fallen? Here?

ASA. Probably.

STEPHEN HASTINGS. And where is my finger? What part of the bed?

ASA. The middle.

STEPHEN HASTINGS. And what was in the middle of the bed the night your son was born.

ASA. My wife.

STEPHEN HASTINGS. What part of your wife? Her torso?

ASA. Yes.

STEPHEN HASTINGS. Thank you. Do you remember what Sibyl was wearing that night?

ASA. I think she was wearing a sweater and blue jeans. A heavy sweater.

STEPHEN HASTINGS. Do you remember what color it was?

ASA. No, sir.

STEPHEN HASTINGS. Your Honor, Defense's number three for identification. Is this the sweater Sibyl was wearing?

ASA. I think so.

STEPHEN HASTINGS. What color is it?

ASA. Navy blue.

STEPHEN HASTINGS. Reverend Bedford, we've established that your son was born sometime between six-fifteen and six-twenty in the morning. Did you sleep at all the night before?

ASA. No, I didn't.

STEPHEN HASTINGS. So you'd been up all night when your son was born. Were your eyes tired?

ASA. I don't remember thinking they were.

STEPHEN HASTINGS. Might they have been?

TANNER. Objection.

JUDGE DORSET. I'll allow it.

STEPHEN HASTINGS. After being awake for twenty-four hours, might your eyes have been tired?

ASA. It's possible.

STEPHEN HASTINGS. Thank you. Now, you've told the court that you think you may have seen this bit of blood spurt, despite the fact that you were almost eight feet away when it happened. Correct?

ASA. Yes.

STEPHEN HASTINGS. And despite the fact that your wife's stomach was covered in shadow. Correct?

ASA. Yes.

STEPHEN HASTINGS. And despite the fact that you would have been seeing this blood against a navy blue backdrop. Right?

ASA. Yes.

STEPHEN HASTINGS. And despite the fact that you had been awake for a full twenty-four hours. Is that the testimony you want this jury to believe?

ASA. I know what I saw.

STEPHEN HASTINGS. Did you believe your wife was dead when you went to the window?

ASA. Yes.

STEPHEN HASTINGS. Did you love her?

ASA. Of course.

STEPHEN HASTINGS. Were you sad?

ASA. Good Lord, yes!

STEPHEN HASTINGS. And it was in that frame of mind that you think you saw blood spurt?

ASA. Yes, but I was not hysterical. I know what I saw.

STEPHEN HASTINGS. And yet, did you make any effort—any effort at all—to stop Sibyl when you saw the blood?

ASA. No, as I told Mr. Tanner, I thought it was normal. I assumed Charlotte had passed away and this was just . . . just what the body did.

STEPHEN HASTINGS. No further questions, Your Honor.

SIBYL. Can I ask you something?

CONNIE. Sure.

SIBYL. At that point, the State rests its case, you've been sitting there for the entire "assault," as you call it—

CONNIE. That's what it was.

SIBYL. Okay, then why didn't it work?

CONNIE. What do you mean?

SIBYL. You'd been listening to that stuff for six days and you still didn't have any doubts?

CONNIE. Why are you doing this?

SIBYL. I'm just trying to put myself in your place.

CONNIE. Well, stop. I'm already here. No, I didn't have any doubts and if I had, Stephen's case would have brought me back to my senses.

ROAD CREW MAN. Wasn't anything moving 'fore we got there with the sand.

PHONE WOMAN. Due to the storm, phone service was interrupted at 12:15 A.M. and was not restored until—

FORENSIC SPECIALIST. The tires had burned down into the ice, but not enough to create any real traction. The vehicle was turned at a thirty-degree—

PHYSICIAN. This anterior view of the right leg shows that Mrs. Danforth suffered multiple cuts and contusions to the knee and shin. I call your attention to the swelling—

SIBYL. Yes, the weather was awful, but there was nothing in their testimony to undermine Tanner's point that I should never have been trapped with the Bedfords in the first place.

CONNIE. Which is why Stephen followed up with the character witnesses. If they wanted to question your judgement, they'd have to get past people like Lori and David Pine first.

LORI. Why would we have all five of our children with the same midwife if we didn't have absolute faith in her ability?

DAVID. No matter what, you knew she was competent.

MOLLY. Always so careful.

RITA. You could tell she cared.

LORI. Highly respected by her peers.

MOLLY. So popular, she had to refer new mothers to me.

RITA. Always keeping records, checking her notes.

DAVID. The woman would spend fifteen minutes just washing her hands.

MOLLY. You always know exactly where you stand with Sibyl.

LORI. She turned to me and said, "Lori, I think you'd be better off in a hospital this time."

DAVID. And that was that.

TANNER. You really have no idea what you're talking about then, do you?

BARTON. Oh, I think I do. I think I understand how a labor develops and—

TANNER. *This* labor. Not any labor. This labor.

BARTON. I understood your question.

TANNER. You never met Charlotte. You never saw her body after her death. You never saw her records. Why do you feel you understand her death so well?

BARTON. Think about it now, I'm the woman's backup doctor. I haven't had a conversation with an ob-gyn in the last six months where this case hasn't come up.

TANNER. But you know nothing firsthand, do you?

BARTON. Mr. Tanner, I have known Sibyl for close to a decade. She has a more complete knowledge of labor and delivery than almost any person I know, including many of the so-called experts we listened to last week. . . . Sibyl Danforth tells me the woman was dead when she did the C-section, in my mind the case is closed.

CONNIE. When you finally took the stand, it was clear you were exhausted, but you had this peaceful, heroic look— like it was all up to God now.

SIBYL. If I see a danger, I will never let a mother's desire to have her baby at home cloud my judgement. If there are any indications that the baby is in distress, I will transfer the woman to the hospital. Period.

CONNIE. You were solid all morning, talking about Charlotte

and then about the birth. Later though, when you'd been on the stand for almost three hours, I could tell you were losing focus.

SIBYL. I didn't ask Asa in so many words, "May I save the baby?" and maybe I should have, but at the time I was focused on the baby and that conversation seemed unnecessary.

STEPHEN HASTINGS. Am I correct in saying that conversation was unnecessary because in your opinion Asa understood exactly what you were planning to do and had therefore given his consent?

TANNER. Objection. Leading the witness, Your Honor.

JUDGE DORSET. Sustained.

CONNIE. Just after that you came out with something that was definitely not part of the script. I mean, this was the opposite of what you actually believe.

STEPHEN HASTINGS. Did the father try to stop you?

SIBYL. Asa was a husband as well as a father, and no husband in that situation would be in any condition to make that kind of decision.

STEPHEN HASTINGS. But in your judgement he made a . . . conscious decision not to stop you, correct?

SIBYL. Correct.

CONNIE. By now you were obviously struggling. I knew something had to give.

STEPHEN HASTINGS. And the father was still beside the window?

SIBYL. Yes, he was sitting in the chair there, holding his baby in his arms, and Anne was right beside him. From where they were, I knew they couldn't see the . . . incision, and I was glad. I don't recall actually turning out the light when I was through, but I looked at my journal the other day and I saw that I had.

STEPHEN HASTINGS. . . . You mean your medical journal?

SIBYL. No. My personal journal. My diary.

TANNER. . . . Your Honor, may I approach the bench?

> *(STEPHEN HASTINGS and TANNER consult with JUDGE DORSET.)*

CONNIE. It's not like it was illegal. We were under no obligation to tell the State that you had a personal journal.

SIBYL. Stephen read a little of it once. He warned me to stop writing and he said not to mention it again until after the trial. But I'd kept a journal since my early twenties. So now, during the most excruciating experience of my life, I was supposed to just stop?

JUDGE DORSET. The Court orders that Mrs. Danforth's journal be brought to me by the end of lunch, at which time I will review the material in my chambers. I will decide what, if anything, is relevant.

STEPHEN HASTINGS. Sibyl, I want to keep you up on the stand until noon, okay? We'll get you rested up for cross-examination over lunch.

SIBYL. Fine. That's . . .What about the journal?

STEPHEN HASTINGS. I'll have one of my aides drive out to get it. *(Calling off.)* Peter!

SIBYL. How will he know where to look?

CONNIE. I can go with him. If you want. I know right where it is.

SIBYL. You must have thought I'd lost my mind.

CONNIE. I did wonder, driving out, I mean it did cross my mind that maybe you'd given up. Just wanted it to end. Subconsciously even. . . . Then I thought, wait a minute. *My* mother? Giving up? She's going to let these people slander us, and slander her profession?

SIBYL. They wanted me in jail, Connie. It wasn't face I was trying to save, it was family.

CONNIE. That's what I realized. I got home and I ran into your office and that's when it hit me that, no, you would do anything in your power to keep us together. I decided I would do the same.

> *(Split scene: CONNIE uses a razor knife to slice select pages from the journal. STEPHEN HASTINGS and SIBYL are at lunch.)*

STEPHEN HASTINGS. Anything else? Anything.

SIBYL. I don't know, I may have written something about . . . no, that was . . . No. Nothing as bad as the March 15th entry.

STEPHEN HASTINGS. Okay, so . . . New strategy.

SIBYL. You have a strategy for this?

STEPHEN HASTINGS. Otherwise I'd be the defense-less attorney. From now on, the fact is it doesn't matter whether you thought Charlotte was alive or not; our forensic and obstetric experts are positive the woman was dead.

SIBYL. I'm just a midwife, is that it?

STEPHEN HASTINGS. I didn't say it was flattering. . . . I would like your consent, though.

SIBYL. You do what you have to. It won't change what happened.

STEPHEN HASTINGS. Thank you. Now, you are about to be cross-examined by one of the nastier State's Attorneys of the century.

SIBYL. So what's my strategy?

STEPHEN HASTINGS. We get some soup into you, you get your strength up . . . then you go tear that son of a bitch a new perineum.

JUDGE DORSET. The Court rules that there is nothing in Mrs. Danforth's diary that is relevant to this case. It is a personal account of her life and will not be shared with the State.

SIBYL. Boom. Just like that, and it was essentially over. There were occasional sparks during my cross-examination, though I don't think I administered the episiotomy Stephen had in mind. . . . On Thursday, our experts all said in one way or another that I had not killed Charlotte Bedford. On Friday, the attorneys gave their closing arguments, the jury began their deliberation by lunch, and by four that afternoon we were back in court to hear the verdict.

JUDGE DORSET. Would the Foreman please review the envelope with the forms? . . . Are those the forms you signed and are they in order?

FOREMAN. They are.

> *(In a split scene, we see CONNIE slipping the severed pages back into the journal.)*

SIBYL. Where is she?

STEPHEN HASTINGS. What?

JUDGE DORSET. Will the defendant please stand and face the jury?

SIBYL. Where's Connie? She should be back.

STEPHEN HASTINGS. Stand up.

FOREMAN. Of the charge of practicing medicine without a license, we find the defendant guilty.

SIBYL. I don't understand.

STEPHEN HASTINGS. We expected that.

SIBYL. I mean about Connie.

FOREMAN. Of the charge of involuntary manslaughter, we find the defendant not guilty.

> *(MIDWIVES swarm SIBYL.)*

FOREMAN. *(To an INTERVIEWER, as the court empties.)* We all knew the judge was reading her journal during the recess—that was clear. And so we expected we'd get to hear what she'd written. But I guess he didn't see anything incriminating in it. I can't speak for anyone else, but that mattered a lot to me.

> *(CONNIE and SIBYL sit silently in the hospital room. The IV has been removed. SIBYL has a small bandage on her inner arm.)*

SIBYL. Where *did* you go?

CONNIE. During the verdict? . . . I knew I was going to start blubbering, so I just stayed in the restroom . . . blubbering. . . . But I knew what it was going to be, I wasn't surprised.

SIBYL. I had no idea . . .

CONNIE. Well, it's probably good we talked about it. We've never really . . . Anyway, I feel better. . . . How 'bout you? *(Pause.)*

LOUISE. *(Entering.)* All right you two, I've gotta move you out to the low-rent district. Got another customer coming in. A managed care executive, how's that for irony? *(To SIBYL.)* How you doin', you got your sea legs?

SIBYL. Look at me, I'm up. I'm fine.

LOUISE. We'll get you set up out in reception, you can stay as long as you like. . . . Don't forget your book there. *(CONNIE grabs the journal. Loose pages float to the floor.)* Oops, you're fallin' apart there. *(CONNIE tries to slip them back, but SIBYL takes them from her. She reads one, then stares, dumbstruck, at CONNIE.)* I'll go tell my executive it's gonna be another five, okay? . . . Maybe ten. *(LOUISE exits.)*

SIBYL. Stephen was the only other person who read those pages. He warned me, he said, they're too honest, Sibyl. People aren't used to that much honesty. That much self-doubt. . . . I used to think, that's where strength came from. Daring to doubt myself. My perceptions. Now I see that I've infected you with it. You're riddled with my doubt. My crimes.

CONNIE. Mom, we didn't do anything wrong. We saved that little boy.

SIBYL. No, Connie. I did that. Right or wrong, I opened that woman up. And now, you seem to think that you can make up for my actions by performing that same operation yourself, over and over. . . . Tell me that I'm guilty.

CONNIE. No.

SIBYL. Tell me that I killed Charlotte Bedford.

CONNIE. I don't think that.

SIBYL. I don't believe you.

CONNIE. Well I can't help that.

SIBYL. Yes you can. *(SIBYL holds up one of the journal entries.)* Read it.

CONNIE. Mom, I'm not going—

SIBYL. Read it to me.

CONNIE. Mom.

SIBYL. That's all I ask. . . . Then we'll go.

> *(CONNIE sits. During the following SIBYL stands behind, rubbing CONNIE'S back, supporting her. Sound of FREEZING RAIN fades up.)*

CONNIE. "March 15, 1981. . . . The room was really quiet, it was like even the ice and snow had stopped banging against the window. For a second I was aware of this chattering and I looked around and figured that Asa and Anne must have heard it too. But they didn't, because it was in my head. It was my teeth."

SIBYL. Good.

CONNIE. "I looked down at my hands, and they were trembling so badly the knife was shaking. And so I inhaled . . ."

SIBYL. Okay . . .

CONNIE. "Really slowly and exhaled. When I cut into Charlotte I didn't want to be shaking so much I couldn't control the knife and accidentally nick the baby."

SIBYL. You can do it.

CONNIE. "Then I just did it." I can't.

SIBYL. Yes you can.

CONNIE. I . . . "I pushed the tip of the knife firmly into the skin."

SIBYL. Go on. "I don't think anyone . . ."

CONNIE. "I don't think anyone but me—" NO! *(CONNIE throws the page to the floor.)*

SIBYL. Connie, you can do this. *(SIBYL holds the page in front of CONNIE.)* You can do it.

CONNIE. *(Soberly, eyes closed, from memory.)* "I don't think anyone but me saw the body flinch. At the time, I just thought it was one of those horrible postmortem reflexes that you hear about in animals. . . ."

SIBYL. I thought the same thing—

CONNIE. "I thought the same thing when there was all that blood, and it just kept flowing and flowing. After all, I'd checked for a pulse and I'd checked for a heartbeat and there hadn't been one. How could she be alive? But looking back on it now, after I've had some sleep, I just don't know. Whenever I think of that flinch . . . I just don't know."

> *(CHARLOTTE is now visible in the half-light.)*

SIBYL. There.

CONNIE. Mama, I don't care what happened, you did what you thought was right.

SIBYL. So did you.

CONNIE. And I really do, I want to be a baby catcher, but . . . I want to be like Barton. I want to be an ob-gyn who understands about home birth. Who helps.

SIBYL. I believe you . . .

CONNIE. Because what happened to you, that's rare. That never, almost never, ever happens.

SIBYL. I still say it never did. . . . Look, you left out a part.

CONNIE. What? No I didn't.

SIBYL. Really.

CONNIE. Where?

SIBYL. "I'd checked for a pulse and I'd checked for a heartbeat." Start there.

CONNIE. "I'd checked for a pulse and I'd checked for a heartbeat, and there hadn't been one. So how could she be alive? The fact is, she couldn't, and she wasn't. That's what I thought as I drew the knife down, and I know I was . . ."

SIBYL & CONNIE. "Absolutely sure of it then."

CONNIE. You were absolutely sure.

SIBYL. Yes.

CONNIE. Then so am I.

> (SIBYL and CONNIE watch CHARLOTTE disappear into the dark. FREEZING RAIN continues.)

END OF PLAY

About the Author

Dana Yeaton is the winner of the Heideman Award from the Actor's Theatre of Louisville. His most recent play, *Mad River Rising*, won the 1998 Moss Hart Award and has just been nominated for a Bessie Award. Other recent plays include *JUMP CUT,* a one-man video-theatre piece produced at Burlington's Flynn Theatre, and *To Bed With Betsy,* a full-length farce produced at the Volkov Theatre in Yaroslavl, Russia, that country's oldest professional theatre. His dark comedy *Lousy Mothers* was winner of a New Play Fellowship at the Shenandoah International Playwrights Retreat in Virginia.

Yeaton is the author of many plays for young adults, including *Democracy Rules! A Rally for Activism, Garden of Needham,* and *Alice in Love,* winner of the 1993 Vermont State Drama Festival. He has received three fellowships in playwriting from the Vermont Arts Council. Currently he teaches dramatic writing at Middlebury College and directs the Vermont Young Playwrights Project, which he founded in 1994.

About PenStroke Press

PenStroke Press is a student publishing venture that was initiated at Rochester High School in September of 1997 through a grant from the Randolph Regional School-to-Work Consortium, with additional funding from the Vermont Arts Council Partners-in-Education grant. The press is a partnership project between Rochester High School and two professional publishing companies—Inner Traditions International and Schenkman Books.

PenStroke Press thanks Webcom printing company of Toronto, Canada, a member of the Vermont Book Professionals Association, for their continuing community outreach support, and Castleton State College, which helped to underwrite the cost of printing this book.